# Prophets, Priests, and Kings: A New Way to Consider Spiritual Gifts

# Prophets, Priests, and Kings: A New Way to Consider Spiritual Gifts

*Doing the Greater Works of Christ in the Church*

GABE SYLVIA

WIPF & STOCK · Eugene, Oregon

PROPHETS, PRIESTS, AND KINGS: A NEW WAY TO CONSIDER SPIRITUAL GIFTS
Doing the Greater Works of Christ in the Church

Copyright © 2024 Gabe Sylvia. All rights reserved. Except for brief quotations in critical publications or reviews, no part of this book may be reproduced in any manner without prior written permission from the publisher. Write: Permissions, Wipf and Stock Publishers, 199 W. 8th Ave., Suite 3, Eugene, OR 97401.

Wipf & Stock
An Imprint of Wipf and Stock Publishers
199 W. 8th Ave., Suite 3
Eugene, OR 97401

www.wipfandstock.com

PAPERBACK ISBN: 978-1-6667-7116-9
HARDCOVER ISBN: 978-1-6667-7117-6
EBOOK ISBN: 978-1-6667-7118-3

01/04/24

This book is dedicated to my beloved wife, Kim. For three decades (and counting) you have been a faithful partner and friend, a patient helper and support, a wise counselor and comforter. The author's name is mine yet so much credit belongs to you.

I love you and am thankful to the Lord for you, Kim.

And, as the first and the last, to the Lord Jesus Christ. To you, O Lord, belongs the glory and fame and honor if there should be any who profit from these words. Forgive me, Lord, for they do not give You what You deserve—yet I offer them to You nonetheless. You are my portion now and forever (Lamentations 3:24).

# Contents

Preface | ix
Acknowledgments | xiii
Introduction: Prophets, Priests, and Kings | xv

*Part One | The Need*
1   Spiritual Gift Assessments and Why They Aren't Very Helpful | 3

*Part Two | Typology Trajectory*
2   Theological Framework for the Prophet-Priest-King Paradigm: The Use of Typology | 23
3   Jesus the Messiah: Archetype Prophet, Priest, and King | 38
4   The Promise and Provision of "Greater Works" | 67

*Part Three | The Paradigm in Action*
5   The Practice of "Greater Works" | 103
6   The PPK Model for Local Church Ministry | 124
7   Conclusion | 155

Bibliography | 159

# Preface

HONESTLY, I HAVE NEVER liked spiritual gift assessments. That's how this all began. Years ago when I was in seminary in Deerfield, Illinois, a friend of mine put me on to biblical counseling. In the course of my reading, I discovered a claim that spiritual gift assessments were somehow related to psychology—specifically the Myers-Briggs Type Indicator tool. Flabbergasted, I decided then and there I'd never touch another assessment!

With time (and growth out of a theological "cage stage"), I came back around and recognized *some* of their usefulness. Still, since I was converted in 1989, my faith journey has included Pentecostal, Baptist, and (now) Presbyterian churches. Along the way, I have taken several spiritual gift assessments. As I reflect on these experiences, I was confused as to why they often gave me a different "gift" result. Or, even why the assessments were often so different from one another. Over time, some of my skepticism about their helpfulness returned.

As that happened, my interest in developing a means to help the church both discover and deploy ourselves according to spiritual gifting increased. For years I had been asking if spiritual gift inventories were the only way to do it?

It is John Calvin I "blame" now. Several years ago, I took a class on Calvin from Dr. Derek Thomas at Reformed Theological Seminary in Charlotte, North Carolina. In reading the *Institutes of the Christian Religion*, I discovered Calvin's view that the church does our ministry work (i.e., spiritual gifts' work) in a way analogous to the Lord's work, that is, in the offices of prophet, priest, and

*Preface*

king.[1] We don't do the work *just* like He did, of course, but *as* He did (I'll explain).

Calvin doesn't develop this in his *Institutes*, though he makes mention of it in his commentaries.[2] Once I saw this in Calvin's writings, I was curious to see if he was alone in this view. I researched further and found he was not alone in the Reformed tradition holding to this view.[3] Still, questions remained:

- What to do with the lists of gifts found in the New Testament: why were they different from each other in length and content?
- Were these lists meant to be combined and thereby constitute an exhaustive list?
- What about gifted saints found in the Old Testament (e.g., Bezalel: Exod 31:3)—how are they connected to the spiritually gifted in the New Testament?

Investigating these questions and others have led me to develop a biblical framework for understanding and engaging in local church ministry: it is as prophets, priests, and kings.

In the chapters that follow, I start with an analysis of spiritual gift assessments and give them a proper burial. Then, I build the biblical case for understanding giftedness in terms of prophets, priests, and kings (PPK).[4] This culminates in presenting the "Prophet, Priest, and King Assessment" (PPKa). Through a series of sixty questions, the user can determine which of the three areas is primary with a mechanism also to understand how the two other roles interact with it. This includes instruction on external verification as well as suggested areas of ministry depending on which role is primary.

1. Calvin, *Institutes*, 496, 500, 502.
2. For example, *Commentary on a Harmony of the Evangelists*, 228.
3. I lay this out further in chapter 8 my unpublished DMIN dissertation, "Local Church Ministry According to the Ancient Paradigm of Prophets, Priests and Kings," accepted at Reformed Theological Seminary, Charlotte, North Carolina, 2021.
4. In Latin, the *munus triplex*.

*Preface*

My hope is that the PPKa will be useful to pastors and church leaders in better identifying and deploying their church members in ministry—SDG.

Heaven soon,
Pastor Gabe Sylvia

# Acknowledgments

THIS PROJECT IS THE end of a journey that began in 2004. It was then I suggested to my dear wife, Kim, that I'd like to pursue a doctorate for my own growth and (hopefully) the edification of God's church. From the outset, Kim has been a faithful prayer partner, supporter, and friend. Countless times I squirrelled myself away to research and write—sometimes at home and sometimes away. Kim was always encouraging, hopeful, and almost as determined to see this project come to term as I was. I could not have finished without her support. Thank you, my love. Next to our wonderful Savior, Jesus Christ, you are the most blessed gift I have ever received. I love you.

I also want to thank my children: Kelsey, Luke, Noelle, Liberty, and Abigail. At first they didn't understand what Dad was working on, but eventually they grew to know and to kindly allow me the time to work as I needed. My hope was to make them proud to be PKs (in more ways than one)—I hope this helps! Along the way, they have inquired about the progress and encouraged me to strive on to its end. You are all very dear to me. I love you and thank you.

To this list, I need to add my mom, Marilyn Walling Hawkins. She has been a supporter of my pursuit of ministry for many years. Recently, she spent hours pouring over this manuscript catching many things that escaped me. Mom, your friendship and support have been greatly treasured over the years. My hope is that many are led to Christ as a result of your investments and prayers. Thank you so much. Love you.

## Acknowledgments

Finally, I wish to thank the pastors and elders of the churches I have served along the way: Trinity Presbyterian Church (Orangeburg, SC), Christ Covenant Church (Matthews, NC), and Christ Our Hope Church (Wake Forest, NC). John Ropp, Mike Ross, Bernie Lawrence, Bruce Creswell, Brian Peterson, and Tim Sharpe: all colleagues, encouragers, counselors, and friends. Thank you, brothers, for encouraging and sharpening me along the way.

To the men of the sessions of these churches—especially Ozzie Fogle, Jim Sutton, Wade Byrum, Bob Goudzwaard, Paul Joyce, Jim Pendergrass, Don Allard, Mike Brooks, Mike Anderson, Michael Ovack, and Wynn Baum. You brothers have been patient as I periodically stepped away from church responsibilities to research and write. You have generously assisted me with resources and helpfully and consistently prayed for me along the way. Eventually I came to see this project as a means to serve you and the churches you shepherd. Thank you, brothers, for having vision that allowed me to pursue this project. May God richly bless each of you.

# Introduction: Prophets, Priests, and Kings

MISSION. WORK. IN THE church we like to connect these two words especially in the springtime when churches invite their supported missionaries home to tell their stories. I remember being stirred by the stories of the missionaries; after listening to the power of the gospel to save the lost, it is hard to resist the urge to pack a suitcase and go! World mission is the charge of the church, yet, at the same time, it is important to recognize "mission work," that is, making disciples into worshiping churches (Matt 28:18–20), is the charge of every church. How do we do it? That's the burden of this book. To be sure, this includes missions in the traditional sense of mission conferences, missionaries, or mission agencies. Yet, seeing "mission" in only those terms truncates what is otherwise a grander purpose God has for the church.

If we want to understand how we are to make worshipers, we need look no further than the opening chapters of God's word. From the first verses of Scripture we read that God Himself is on the mission of making worshipers, that is, to call out and build up a people for Himself. Genesis, as well as the rest of God's Word, progressively unfolds the manner in which He does this. We note a three-fold approach. The first is found in Gen 1:28:

> And God blessed them. And God said to them, "Be fruitful and multiply and fill the earth and subdue it, and have dominion over the fish of the sea and over the birds of

## Introduction: Prophets, Priests, and Kings

the heavens and over every living thing that moves on the earth."[1]

The mission given to Adam and Eve (and affirmed again to Noah in Gen 9) was to populate, build, oversee, and govern. They were given "vice-regency" in creation where mankind would serve as the overseers of it. To rule over all creation as God's chosen stewards, for now, we'll consider a "kingly" mission.[2] Through this kingly mission, humanity was to pursue fruitfulness and dominion under God's eye.

The second way is introduced in Gen 2:8, 15:

> And the LORD God planted a garden in Eden, in the east, and there He put the man whom He had formed . . . the LORD God took the man and put him in the garden of Eden to work it and keep it.

At first glance, this appears to be simply an extension of the kingly mission, and, indeed, the two can't be separated. However, to "work" and "keep" is progressively unpacked in Scripture describing the work of the priest in service to God and man.[3] This was a "priestly" role Adam had received from the Lord, and he was to exercise it on behalf of his family as their representative.[4]

The third way of the mission is implicit in the creation narrative and made more explicit in the lives of the patriarchs (e.g., Gen 18:19) and down through the ages of God's people. The Lord instructed Adam saying,

---

1. Unless otherwise indicated, all Scripture quotations are from the English Standard Version.

2. Breshears, "Body of Christ," 7. See also Belcher, *Genesis*, 57. This mission was affirmed (with modifications) in the covenant God made with Noah: Gen 8:20–9:7.

3. Belcher, *Genesis*, 62–63. He writes, "The implication [of our work according to God's appointment in the Garden] is that the purpose of work is more than an activity that allows a person to provide for his needs but that work is a vocation which enables a person to fulfill a calling of service to others and to God."

4 See Beale and Carson, *Temple and the Church's Mission*.

## Introduction: Prophets, Priests, and Kings

You may surely eat of every tree of the garden but of the tree of the knowledge of good and evil you shall not eat for in the day that you eat of it you shall surely die (Gen 2:16–17).

What would later be evident in the story is the man's responsibility to pass on the instruction of the Lord first to his wife, Eve, and then to their children.[5] To deliver the Word of God as His messenger is later identified as the "prophet's" role.[6]

## THE CHALLENGE TO THE WORK: THE FALL

The framework to accomplish the mission of God was by these three roles or offices: prophets, priests, and kings (PPK). In the pristine garden, humanity's experience of these would be unhindered: vice-regents of the Lord (king), serving Him in the temple Garden (priest) and proclaiming His word to the generations (prophet).

Yet, tragically Adam and Eve chose to follow another voice in the garden, and that decision has had abiding impact on this threefold mission. For example, the kings' work was crippled. While the kingly mandate to be fruitful and have dominion in some form persists (e.g., Gen 5:1–2; 9:1, 6–7), now populating and filling the earth would always be accompanied by pain and relational strife (Gen 3:16). Also, cursed is the ground only giving up its produce through toil and hardship (Gen 3:17–19).

But also with this came estrangement—the priests' work was now broken. The holiness of God now made Him an enemy to the unholiness in His people (Gen 3:24). Gone was the time when mankind could stroll through the garden in the cool of the day in intimate fellowship with our God (Gen 3:8). Now, the tasks to "work" and "keep" had to be radically modified. Mankind now required new rules and arrangements between God and

---

5. See also Gen 18:19.

6. We do find further explanation of man's original creation as prophets, priests, and kings in the Reformed tradition, particularly Vos, *Reformed Dogmatics*, 86; Berkhof, *Systematic Theology*, 357.

man—preeminently requiring a mediator. As if this wasn't terrible enough, person-to-person relational dynamics were effected so that now our interactions with each other are ordered by sin and violence (Gen 3:12; 9:2–6).

And lastly, the prophets' clarity was dimmed. Adam, whose heart originally was not burdened with sin and fallenness, could know God and follow His word. But, with the fall, our knowledge of God and His will is hidden and suppressed (Rom 1:18ff). With hearts of stone rather than hearts of flesh, our interest in God is cold. Though, man now needs instruction, reproof, and rebuke in order to know of and succeed at the mission of God, he refuses and resists.

## THE WORK CONTINUES: THE GIFTED PEOPLE OF GOD

All is not lost! From Adam's line down through the ages God gave prophets, priests, and kings to His people to accomplish His will.[7] This unfolded first in the Old Testament where God raised up these men among His covenant people who ministered because of the needs of the people and the will of God. Their ministry was essential in its own right yet, importantly, they were also to set the stage for both their archetype,[8] the Lord Jesus Christ, and His ectypes, the local church.[9]

The work of the prophets, priests, and kings of old pointed to the archetypal work of the Lord Jesus. We will consider that movement from type to archetype in more detail below. Yet, before the Lord's declaration, "it is finished" (John 19:30), He said this in John 14:12–14:

---

7. For example, priests: Gen 4:28, 8:20, 12:7, 14:18; kings: Gen 9:1ff; prophets: Gen 18:19. These are simply samples of the presence of the PPK in the people of God.

8. The technical term for this is "anti-type." I use archetype, a less technical term, for clarity.

9. An "ectype" is a reproduction or copy of an original (*American Heritage Dictionary*). Much more on this below!

## Introduction: Prophets, Priests, and Kings

> Truly, truly, I say to you, whoever believes in me will also do the works that I do; and greater works than these will he do, because I am going to the Father. Whatever you ask in my name, this I will do, that the Father may be glorified in the Son. If you ask me anything in my name, I will do it.

The Lord tells His people we still have work to do—work *like* His. How is this work done? In the apostolic letters, we find the Holy Spirit equips the local church from the "top down" for ministry from the "bottom up." This arrangement is explicit in Eph 4:11–12:

> And [the ascended Lord Jesus] gave the apostles, the prophets, the evangelists, the shepherds and teachers, to equip the saints for the work of ministry, for building up the body of Christ.

A first reading of this familiar passage shows the Spirit gives gifted preachers and teachers to the church. These "foundational" gifts or roles serve to train the saints for the work of ministry. The results? As Paul continues, "equipped" saints doing the work of ministry who attain to the "unity of the faith," the "knowledge of the Son of God," "mature manhood," and a measure of Christ's stature in holiness, godliness, and service.

In other words, to do the work the Lord promised we would do, the Holy Spirit empowers a saint to use his or her spiritual gift for the common good. The apostle Paul makes this explicit in 1 Corinthians 12:7: "to each is given the manifestation of the Spirit for the common good."

## A WAY FORWARD

The call to our work (seen, for example in Gen 1–2), the promise of our work (John 14:12–14), the provision for our work (Eph 4:11–12), as well as the practice of it (e.g., 1 Cor 12:7), are straightforward in Scripture. Given these facts, it seems there might exist widely used practical tools to develop and deploy the church in all

## Introduction: Prophets, Priests, and Kings

of this. Unfortunately, beside the recent development of spiritual gift inventories, there is no widespread practical tool in use across Christendom to identify and leverage the Spirit's gifts in a way that propels us forward in our mission. That there is no standard or universal tool certainly does not mean the mission of God is faltering! It is simply to suggest it isn't thriving as it is designed to thrive.

As we saw above, Jesus tells His disciples with His departure and the coming of the Holy Spirit, we will do His works and "greater works." This has implications we will unpack in depth. But, first, let's go back to the spiritual gifts assessments. In the course of my research, I took five of them and I lay out the results below. We start there because, quite frankly, I want to give them a proper burial.

# PART ONE

*The Need*

# PART ONE

## The Novel

# CHAPTER ONE

## Spiritual Gift Assessments and Why They Aren't Very Helpful

IT IS GOOD TO be specific, right? ". . . aren't very helpful" is an important turn of phrase. It is not as if the church has failed in its mission over the two millennia since Pentecost! Indeed, the faithfulness of God has been clearly evident through the ages. At the same time, as these ages draw near to the return of the Lord, the need for an organized approach to this ministry is both reasonable and important. And, I contend, in our post-Christian culture, some of the approaches of the recent modern era (including spiritual gift assessments) seem outdated and are perhaps now ineffective.

This chapter will begin our study with a brief history of the work of the church through spiritual gifts. Additionally, to sustain my contention that a different approach to church work is needed, namely using the "Prophet, Priest, and King" framework, I submitted to several of these instruments to yield the results they recommended. What I will show through my results is the variability from one instrument to the next, the confusion it potentially causes the test-taker, and the marginal usefulness they provide.[1]

---

1. I recognize these results are anecdotal yet I believe they illustrate the challenges inherent in these instruments. For my analysis, see below.

Part One | The Need

# A (VERY) BRIEF HISTORY SPIRITUAL GIFT ASSESSMENTS

We have already introduced the concepts of the "provision" (Eph 4:11–12) and the "practice" (e.g., 1 Cor 12:7) of local church ministry. These ideas are hardly new; the Scripture indicates these represent the ordinary way local church ministry should be organized. Regarding spiritual gifts as part of that effort, the church, in its history, has had two basic approaches to this: gifts-neutral and gifts-engaging.

Most of the history of the church to the late nineteenth century could be considered gifts-neutral.[2] On the one hand, there was a sort of benign neglect of the gifts, as David Hocking points out, "However, the sum total of [early church] references to spiritual gifts leads us to conclude that they were not highly emphasized."[3] On the other, if spiritual gifts were part of the local church ministry, they were mostly considered to be "natural abilities with a touch of spiritual attitude."[4]

This changed in the late nineteenth and early twentieth centuries. With the rise of the Pentecostal movement came new interest in the person and work of the Holy Spirit.[5] With new interest in the Spirit came new interest in the gifts of the Spirit. In America, this interest was mostly confined to Pentecostal circles until the late 1960s, when researchers at Western Conservative Baptist Seminary in Portland, Oregon, led by J. Grant Howard and Earl Radmacher, instituted classes on the spiritual gifts.[6] The first spiritual gifts assessments were created there.[7]

---

2. McIntosh, "Spiritual Gifts Profiles."

3. Hocking, *Spiritual Gifts*, 3. See also Marshall, *Measurement of Spiritual Gifts Using the Modified Houts Questionnaire*, 6–15.

4. McIntosh, "Spiritual Gifts Profiles." C. Peter Wagner briefly lists some exceptions to this but they didn't amount to influential exceptions, Wagner, *Your Spiritual Gifts Can Help Your Church Grow*, 16–18.

5. Hocking, *Spiritual Gifts*, 4.

6. McIntosh, "Spiritual Gifts Profiles"; Wagner, *Spiritual Gifts*, 11–15.

7. McIntosh, "Spiritual Gifts Profiles." These were developed in concert with the MBTI as spiritual extensions of it.

## Spiritual Gift Assessments and Why They Aren't Very Helpful

Around the same time, C. Peter Wagner, a missionary in Bolivia, witnessed the explosive growth of Pentecostal churches there and in Chile. Upon leaving his role to take a post as Professor of Church Growth at the Fuller School of World Mission at Fuller Theological Seminary, Wagner researched and then wrote on spiritual gifts at the local church level. His first edition book was titled *Your Spiritual Gifts Can Help Your Church Grow*. It was published in 1974.[8] As a result of Wagner's work, as well as that of the researchers at Western Conservative Baptist Seminary, the interest in spiritual gift identification and deployment grew significantly.[9]

### CONSIDERATION OF ASSESSMENTS AND SURVEYS

Since Wagner and Hocking wrote their books, the Western church has leaned more "gifts-engaging," mostly using spiritual gift assessments (or inventories) as the means to do it. Indeed, inventories or assessments *have* a place in determining and deploying gifts. Most have solid definitions of the gifts, ask straightforward questions, and ask participants to answer questions based on common sense criteria such as "Never true of me" to "Always true of me"[10] or simply "Y" if it "fits you."[11] Still, as I will show below in my analysis of several gift assessments, they have significant shortcomings.

### "Wagner-Modified Houts" assessment

This venerable instrument has been in use since 1976. C. Peter Wagner made modifications to the original and included it in his book, *Your Spiritual Gifts Can Help Grow Your Church*. It includes 135 diagnostic questions asking "to what extent it is true in your life." The answer choices are: "Much," "Some," "Little" or "Not at

---

8. McIntosh, "Spiritual Gifts Profiles."
9. Wagner, *Spiritual Gifts*, 11–12.
10. "Spiritual Gifts Test."
11. Hocking, *Spiritual Gifts*, 143.

## Part One | The Need

all." Users are told to answer on the basis of past experiences.[12] In taking this assessment, my top three scoring gifts were: "pastor," "teaching," and "administration."[13]

### "SHAPE" assessment

This eighty-four-question instrument is designed to measure more than spiritual gifts. It incorporates other aspects of a person in determining where he should serve in the local church. We see this in the acronym itself. It tests for Spiritual gifts, Heart, Abilities, Personality style, and Experience. It originated at Saddleback Community Church and is currently administered by Solano Beach Presbyterian Church (www.sbpcshape.org). Users are told to answer the questions on the basis of what "most resonates with your personal experiences in serving or that you think best describes you."[14] The answer choices are along the spectrum of "Not at all" to "Always." As noted in its name, the instrument incorporates questions that it connects to a user's passion, abilities, and experiences. Using the SHAPE assessment, my top three scoring gifts were: "teaching," "prophecy," and "administration."

### Spiritualgiftstest.com assessment

This test contains 105 statements rather than questions. In the blanks accompanying the statements, using an accuracy scale, the user is to rate the statement from "Very Inaccurate" to "Very Accurate." The accuracy scale is designed to address your giftedness, "According to who you are, not who you would like to be or should be."[15] The results of the online test rank your gifts out of

---

12. Wagner, *Spiritual Gifts*, 213–217.
13. My second three were wisdom, knowledge and leadership.
14. http://www.sbpcshape.org/PS-Page1.
15. Test taken on 12/14/2020.

*Spiritual Gift Assessments and Why They Aren't Very Helpful*

fifteen gifts.[16] My top three scoring gifts: apostleship, leadership, and teaching.[17]

## Giftstest.com assessment

This assessment has sixty-six statements. It gives no descriptions or guidelines in taking it. Each statement is evaluated using a scale from "Never" to "Always."[18] My top three scoring gifts: teaching, prophecy, and faith.

## Spiritualgiftassessment.org assessment

This assessment has eighty "statements of belief." The instructions are to "Select the one response you feel best characterizes yourself and place that number in the blank provided beside each item. Do not spend too much time on any one item. Remember, it is not a test. Usually your immediate response is best."[19]

The responses are a range from "Definitely untrue for me" to "Definitely true for me." We are also told, "Some items reflect concrete actions; other items are descriptive traits; and still others are statements of belief."[20] My top three scoring gifts: teaching, administration, and wisdom.

---

16. On the printout from the test results, they do not score for the following gifts: healing, tongue-speaking, tongue interpretation, and miracles. There is no indication why these are not scored.
17. Printed "Spiritual Gifts and Personality Profile."
18. https://giftstest.com/test.
19. https://spiritualgiftsassessment.org.
20. https://spiritualgiftsassessment.org.

# Part One | The Need

## General Overview and Comparison of the Assessments

|   |   | #Q's | #Gifts | Criteria | Scale used |
|---|---|---|---|---|---|
| 1 | W-M Houts | 135 | 28 | What extent the statement is true in your life based on past experiences? | Much, Some, Little, Not at all |
| 2 | SHAPE | 84 | 21 | What most resonates with personal experience OR what best describes you? | Not at all, Always |
| 3 | Spiritualgifts test.com | 105 | 19 | According to who you are not who you want to be or should be | Very Inaccurate, Very accurate |
| 4 | Giftstest.com | 66 | 22 | [Not stated] | Never, Always |
| 5 | Spiritualgifts assessment.org | 80 | 16 | Best characterizes yourself | Definitely untrue, Definitely true |

**Figure 1.**

The general results in Figure 1 give a snapshot of the complexity involved in taking more than one spiritual gift assessment. Note the following variances between the assessments:

- Numbers of diagnostic questions or statements: 66 to 135
- Number of gifts tested for: 16 to 28
- Summary of criteria used: true of your life in the past (W-M Houts, SHAPE) to what best describes you (SHAPE, the rest)
- Summary of scale used: frequency (W-M Houts) to accuracy (all others)

*Spiritual Gift Assessments and Why They Aren't Very Helpful*

## My Top Three Scores Across the Five Assessments

| 1 | Pastor | Teaching | Administration |
|---|---|---|---|
| 2 | Teaching | Prophecy | Administration |
| 3 | Apostleship | Leadership | Teaching |
| 4 | Teaching | Prophecy | Faith |
| 5 | Teaching | Administration | Wisdom |

**Figure 2.**

The variances seen in Figure 1 clearly contributed to the varied results in Figure 2. While I will show overlap in the results below (Figure 4), it is important to see how each test created different results.

According to the instruments, my unique, non-overlapping results include "pastor" (W-M Houts), "prophecy" (SHAPE), "apostleship," "leadership" (spiritualgiftstest.com), "faith" (giftstest.com), and "wisdom" (spiritualgiftsassessment.org). Just using the non-overlapping results, if I were to determine where to serve it would be a place where I could lead, teach, administrate, be prophetic as an apostolic pastor demonstrating faith with wisdom!

## Top Three Overlapping Scores Compiled from the Five Assessments

| 5/5 | Teaching |
|---|---|
| 3/5 | Administration |
| 2/5 | Prophecy |

**Figure 3.**

Still, the point of the assessments is to assist the test taker in finding places to serve the church according to gifting. In other words, I had to take *something* away from my efforts! I decided I'd limit the field to the top three scores in each assessment and go from there. In Figure 3 I show the results from the five assessments. As we can see teaching was in each inventory's top three, "administration" was in three assessment's top three, and "prophecy" ranked in the top three in two assessments.[21]

## Teaching

| 1: 2<sup>nd</sup> | 2: 1<sup>st</sup> | 3: 3<sup>rd</sup> | 4: 1<sup>st</sup> | 5: 1<sup>st</sup> |
|---|---|---|---|---|
| "The gift of teaching is the **special ability that God gives** to certain members of the Body of Christ to communicate information relevant *to the health and ministry of the Body and its members* in such a way that others will learn." | "You have a **God-given ability** to effectively gather, organize and clearly <u>explain God's Word</u> in ways that are easily understood so that people can apply the Word in their lives. You are very articulate in connecting Biblical truth to everyday life." | "To <u>teach, instruct, instill doctrine,</u> explain and expound. Those with the gift of teaching love to study the <u>Word of God</u> for extended periods.... They take great joy and satisfaction in seeing others learn and apply the truth of God's Word." | "The gift of teaching is the **divine strength** to study and <u>learn from the Scriptures</u> primarily to bring understanding and depth to *other Christians*." | "<u>Instruct others in the Bible</u> in a logical, systematic way so as to communicate pertinent information for true understanding and growth." |

**Figure 4.**[22]

In this chart, as with the two that follow, we can see the overlap in how the spiritual gift assessments defined the gifts in question. There are two things to note, however. First, there were differences in where this gift ranked in each test. In three tests, teaching was first. In one, second. And in another, third. As I consider how important this gift is in my decision-making about serving, how heavily do I weigh it against others? For example, since three out of five ranked it first, is it first?

21  Figure 2 shows the rest of the results found in each assessment.

22  Similarities between the definitions of the gifts are in font marking. **BOLD** indicates a God-given gift. <u>Underline</u> is the specifics of the gift. *Italics* is the church as recipients of the gift.

*Spiritual Gift Assessments and Why They Aren't Very Helpful*

Secondly, there are additions and omissions in the definitions. We will discuss this in greater depth below. For example, only two tests highlight that teaching is for the body of Christ. Only three of the five explicitly describe the gift as a gift from God. Four of the five specifically say the teaching is of God's Word; one omits it, adding in the teacher is delivering "information relevant to the health and ministry of the Body" (W-M Houts).[23]

## Administration

| 1: 3rd | 2: 3rd | 3: | 4: | 5: 2nd |
|---|---|---|---|---|
| "The gift of administration is the **special ability that God gives** to certain *members of the Body of Christ* to understand clearly the immediate and <u>long-range goals</u> of a particular unity of the Body of Christ and <u>to devise and execute effective plans</u> for the accomplishment of those goals." | "You have a **God-given ability** to understand what makes an organization efficient, and the capacity to <u>plan events, organize information, and implement procedures to accomplish the goals</u> or policies of ministry activities. You are very responsible." | ABSENT | ABSENT | "Steer *God's people* into effective channels of service by understanding the resources needed <u>to accomplish goals and plan, provide direction to others</u> that results in efficient attainment of goals to make plans, launch projects, maintain vision and avoid chaos." |

---

23. Some of these differences could be merely semantic. In other words, written by different groups from different theological backgrounds, some language might be more common to some than others, but in the end they might be targeting the same result. Yet, without a "key" to interpret the differences in language, we are stuck with the complexities.

## Prophecy

| 1: | 2: 3rd | 3: | 4: | 5: 2nd |
|---|---|---|---|---|
| ABSENT | "You have a **God-given ability** to speak God's truth in a relevant and timely way that causes people to return to God and move away from the deceptions that culture can offer. You are compelled to speak the truth, whether it is encouraging or difficult for people to hear. You are very truthful and sometimes controversial." | ABSENT | "The gift of prophecy is the **divine strength** or ability to communicate God's truth and heart in a way that calls people to a right relationship with God." | ABSENT |

## ANALYSIS OF THE CHALLENGES INHERENT IN SPIRITUAL GIFT INVENTORIES

We can see the confusion I faced as a result of these instruments. In the introduction, we saw the provision and practice of local church ministry is equipping from the top-down and ministry from the bottom-up. Scripture gives us this framework from passages such as Eph 4 and 1 Cor 12. Using spiritual gift inventories, churches and Christians have sought to align ministry with this provision and practice.

However, as the results of my own test-taking demonstrated, there are challenges inherent in the usefulness of the inventories. Indeed, there are flaws in their designs that make them questionably useful. I categorize these challenges under two headings: sufficiency and logic.

*Spiritual Gift Assessments and Why They Aren't Very Helpful*

## Challenge #1: Sufficiency

Assessments are normally given as stand-alone instruments. In other words, they aren't administered in conjunction with Bible studies on Ephesians or 1 Corinthians, for example. Beyond surface-level connection with the Holy Spirit[24] (i.e., calling them gifts "of the Spirit"), modern spiritual gift inventories lack meaningful connections to pertinent biblical context or doctrines.

For example, in major evangelical systematic theologies, spiritual gifts are included in sections on ecclesiology[25] or pneumatology.[26] Of course, these are not incorrect as the gifts have direct impact on the church as a whole and they are the work of the Spirit. However, assessments and inventories leave unanswered questions such as: "Why do different books of the New Testament have different lists?" "What's the relationship between the gifts and the finished work of Christ?" "What role do these gifts have in 'building the church?'"[27] "How are these gifts part of the Holy Spirit's overall person and work?" "What role do they have in sanctification?" We can piece together some of the answers to these questions while paging through major systematic theologies, yet those answers aren't often reflected in the design or use of the assessments.

Because the spiritual gifts (especially in the inventories themselves) are not considered in relation to specific biblical contexts or doctrines, they do not give the individual Christian taking the inventories sufficient perspective on the gifts and their relationship to building up the body of Christ, indeed, the continuing work of Christ in the church. For example, in John 14:12–14, Jesus

---

24. In fact, Wagner's book gives no connection to the work of the Holy Spirit and the use of the spiritual gifts. Neither does he address the connection between spiritual gifts and sanctification.

25. Grudem, *Systematic Theology*, 1016–88.

26. Erickson, *Christian Theology*, 865–86.

27. This is the question most often addressed. The answers are often embedded in the definitions or the impact of the gifts themselves. See, for example, Mack and Swavely, *Life in the Father's House*, 158–160, and Hocking, *Spiritual Gifts*, 12–14.

explains the church has work to do that will resemble the work Christ came to do. How do the instruments fit into that scheme? The inventories give either few or insufficient answers.

## Challenge #2: Logic

The more compelling problems with modern spiritual gift inventories have to do with their internal logic. In other words, they normally pursue gift identification, yet due to what I consider flaws in their design, their results are necessarily flawed. There are at least four lines of concern.

### THEOLOGICAL.

First, the theological foundations of the assessments. Each assessment has its own predetermined list of gifts and no two assessments pursue exactly the same list.[28] Most Christians seeking to identify spiritual gifts don't take multiple assessments but some could. And, those who don't wouldn't be confronted with the same issues that confronted me as I was taking multiple assessments. In that case, any underlying theological problems would remain hidden to the test taker.

Or, if some happened to take several instruments as I did, they would be confronted with the strange fact that each inventory pursues a slightly different list of gifts or they use different criteria or they have differing definitions and so forth. Why is this? The test takers are left in the dark. As noted above, the choices of what gifts to test for may be due to a superficial review of gift lists or a lack of coherent connections to biblical doctrines or prior theological concerns.

This also means assessments themselves are already interpretative conclusions. Authors have decided which gifts to include and exclude without providing the decision-making criteria. In

---

28. My own research proved this point. Blogger Tim Challies also makes this observation (Challies, "Spiritual Gift Assessment and the Bible").

## Spiritual Gift Assessments and Why They Aren't Very Helpful

the assessments I took, the list of gifts pursued was as few as sixteen and as many as twenty-eight and I didn't know why. What biblical, doctrinal, or historical data brought test makers to the conclusion that sixteen or twenty-eight gifts was sufficient? Without disclosing how particular gifts came to be included—including the theological perspective behind it—an inventory might either be on shaky biblical grounds or the test taker might not receive an accurate, biblical assessment of his giftedness.[29]

Also, assessments necessarily include conclusions about whether the gift lists are illustrative or exhaustive normally without including the criteria for this choice.[30] Related to the above point, does a test designer include all twenty-one[31] gifts listed in the New Testament passages? Does he dig around in the narratives of Scripture looking for additional examples of men or women who were gifted and include them?[32] These are weighty questions, and just about every assessment has a different answer. Once again, is the choice to include or omit consistent with the Bible and orthodox theology historically defined? And, does the test-taker agree on the methodology?

The instruments act as authoritative guides to the spiritual gifts thereby creating conclusions that can be interpreted as final. Assessments are assumed to be authoritative, giving "final answers" to the important question of "What is my gift?" Indeed, a test-taker might reason, "With so many diagnostic questions, how could the inventory fail to provide an authoritative answer to, 'What is my gift?'" This is a risk in every assessment: the more

---

29. This would even be more complicated if the test taker was, for example, a Presbyterian (like me) and the assessment he took was from a Pentecostal perspective (like C. Peter Wagner's)!

30. Marshall, "Measurement of Spiritual Gifts," 27–31.

31. Compiled omitting gifts that are repeated: Rom 12:6–8 [7], 1 Cor 12:8–10 [8] 28–30 [2], Eph 4:11 [2], 1 Pet 4:10 [2]).

32. Tim Challies does this. He adds the following gifts: "artistry" (Exod 31:1–11), "hospitality" (Rom 12:13), "intercession" (Eph 6:18), "music-vocal" (Ps 96:1–9), "music-instrumental" (Ps 33:1–5), "skilled craft" (Exod 30:1–6) and "writing" (1 John 2:1–6). Challies, "Spiritual Gift Assessment and the Bible. C. Peter Wagner does something similar, *Spiritual Gifts*, 50–52.

detailed the assessment, the more fixed may a person become thinking, "*This* is my gift."[33] This need not be an obstacle to using tools like inventories or assessments, it is simply a risk inherent in them that requires careful design and implementation.

Lastly, prior to the writing of the assessments, gifts are already defined. This *has* to be true: without understanding what answers you're seeking, you won't know what questions to ask. And, as we saw above in Figure 4, different inventories can have differing definitions of the same spiritual gifts. What oversees the definition? The inventories contained different types of definitions. Some stuck closely with lexical or textual definitions[34] while others took interpretative liberty in defining the gifts.[35] The decision the inventory writer makes is his own, however, the final judgment on the definition of a gift is left to the test taker and is he "qualified" to do so?

Accuracy.

The second concern regards the accuracy of the assessment. If a member takes more than one gift inventory (or more than one in a lifetime), then he or she will likely be confronted with a problem of disparate conclusions with no ability to resolve them.[36] Figure 2 above presents a real problem that I have to solve on my own. But how? At this point, do I pick and choose the ones I like? The ones that make me feel best about myself and my work in the church? The ones that appear most frequently? The ones that peers agree with? The ones that mentors agree with?

---

33. Wagner cites Gene Getz who raises this issue in a bullet point, "Some tend to fix their attention on a supposed gift and use it as a rationalization for not fulfilling other biblical responsibilities." *Spiritual Gifts*, 38.

34. www.spiritualgiftstest.com; Hocking, *Spiritual Gifts*.

35. W-M Houts, SHAPE; www.giftstest.com; www.spiritualgiftassessment.org.

36. This actually might naturally occur in a person's lifetime as he grows in the Lord or as she serves different kinds of churches at different times.

## Spiritual Gift Assessments and Why They Aren't Very Helpful

Reading through the definitions the inventories provided, I did find myself resonating more with one than another; do I go with that one even if the other may be more "accurate"? The more self-aware assessments usually provide caveats that the results should be treated tentatively.[37] But that creates another problem on its own: if the assessment's results are tentative, then what's the point of taking it?

### Veracity.

The third concern regards verification of the accuracy of the assessment. Another inherent shortcoming to spiritual gift inventories may be they don't contain a verification process. This is true in two ways. First, most inventories rely on loosely guided self-assessment.[38] Figure 1 demonstrates the varying criteria given to the test taker. On the one hand, I needed to consider what I had done (Wagner-Modified Houts), on the other what best describes me (SHAPE; giftstest.com; spiritualgiftassessment.org).[39] The former is much easier to use to assess a question and provide an answer. But the latter opens the door for much more than objective surveying of past experiences but rather hopes, regrets, and "oughts."

Secondly, once a test is complete, how does one know the answers he's given have led him to the appropriate result? Again, written inventories use language like, "It is strongly suggested that you share these results with someone who knows you well enough to further validate their accuracy."[40] (This is an important step just as verification of "internal call" is part of the ordination process in my denomination.) Still, what questions does the test-taker ask someone to validate the results?

---

37. Wagner, *Spiritual Gifts*, 213; Hocking, *Spiritual Gifts*, 138–142; the printed report from www.spiritualgiftassessment.org.

38. Marshall calls inventories, "self-perception questionnaires," "The Measurement of Spiritual Gifts Using the Modified Houts Questionnaire," 4.

39. The last test found at www.spiritualgiftstest.com gave no criteria.

40. Printed report from www.spiritualgiftassessment.org.

RELIABILITY.

The fourth concern regards the confidence the assessments inspire. Related to above, hammering out answers to the very specific level of a named gift, e.g., "apostle" or "helps" is based on much less specific criteria: "definitely true for me / definitely untrue" or "very accurate / very inaccurate" or "never / always" or "not at all / always" or "Much, Some, Little or None."

Even the groundbreaking assessment, the "Wagner-Modified Houts" assessment comes with the following disclaimer: "You can be confident that it will give you a *fairly accurate* picture of what kind of ministry God expects" and "The 3 or 4 gifts you score highest on *may or may not* turn out to be your real spiritual gifts."[41] Indeed, it seems this is an inherent risk in any assessment and could be why in some churches the inventories aren't as widespread.

## CONCLUSION

In this chapter, I have traced a brief history of spiritual gift identification and deployment. What we have seen is a variety of approaches to local church ministry and consequently a variety of approaches to the identification and use of spiritual gifts in the local church through spiritual gift assessments.

Not only are there differences of philosophy to consider in these, there is an abundance of instruments and assessments to sort through! My own assessment results indicate only modest usefulness. That is, due to the varied theological and methodological commitments in the instruments' design, my results were bound to be uneven. As I noted above, there are other compelling considerations that support my thesis that a more biblically and broadly considered approach is needed.

As I mentioned in the Introduction, the "Prophet, Priest, and King" (PPK) framework is founded in the Old Testament, filtered

---

41. Wagner, *Spiritual Gifts*, 213, italics added. These are incredible statements given the importance Wagner gives to knowing and using one's spiritual gift!

*Spiritual Gift Assessments and Why They Aren't Very Helpful*

through Jesus Christ, and fulfilled in the ministry of the local church. So in the next three chapters, we will engage in hermeneutical as well as exegetical study that further supports these facts. To see the place and usefulness of the PPK in the local church, we need to observe its functioning in the Old Testament and in the ministry of the Lord Jesus. The reason for this is simple: in John 14:12–14, Jesus said the church would continue His ministry.

Therefore, in the next chapter, we'll consider the hermeneutical tool "typology." In that chapter, we'll see the Old Testament types, Jesus as the "anti-type," and the church as ectype. In two chapters that follow, we will dig into several important passages of scripture including those building the doctrine of the person and work of the Holy Spirit and then, in our final chapter, we'll turn to the PPK framework.

# PART TWO

*Typology Trajectory*

# CHAPTER TWO

# Theological Framework for the Prophet-Priest-King Paradigm
## *The Use of Typology*

As I mentioned in the last chapter, one of the big challenges in using the spiritual gift assessments or inventories is they are created and presented as stand-alone instruments. In other words, they aren't designed to be used in connection with biblical or theological doctrines. On the one hand, these instruments see the instruction of Paul in 1 Cor 12:7, and want to take it seriously. So, instrument creators survey the Bible for individuals or gifts that seem connected to the Holy Spirit, mostly in the New Testament, and seek to define the gifts they find and then create tools for saints to evaluate themselves against them. In theory, this is good and potentially helpful.

However, as I mentioned above, the instruments normally pluck the gifts out of their biblical and theological contexts and create tools that may or may not be faithful to where they are found in the Bible or what doctrine they represent. For example, what is the context supporting why Paul spoke to the Corinthian church the way he did in chapter 12 of his first book, and how does that compare to how he addressed the Romans in chapter 12 in its

## Part Two | Typology Trajectory

context? How do these compare to what Peter was doing in 1 Pet 4? And, what is the relationship between Paul's instructions to the Ephesians in chapter 4 to the rest? Unpacking these connections is important to make sure any spiritual gift assessment sits rightly in its biblical and theological place related properly to all the gifts found elsewhere.

This would be a worthy and yet tedious process. However, there is a better way. What we will consider below is the idea that there is something more fundamental that unifies the lists of spiritual gifts and the sprinkling of gifted men and women found in the Bible. In other words, the gift lists themselves are part of a larger theological framework. Considering that larger uniting framework and using it will allow us to also look at the gifted saints and the gift lists and consider them appropriately as ways to serve the local church. That theological framework is the "Prophet, Priest, and King" framework (PPK).

To get at this we will consider the hermeneutical tool of "typology" first. The reason for this is threefold. First, Jesus' words in John 14:12–14 have to be reckoned with: in what sense can Jesus' words be truly worked out? We cannot answer that question without first looking to the work of Christ Himself and, in the history of the church, the mediating work of Christ has been categorized according to the PPK framework, so we need to look even further back in Scripture.[1]

Second, in order for His work to be properly foreshadowed and even recognized, the Lord ordained and commissioned prophets, priests, and kings in the Old Testament. The work of these office-holders captured the core concerns of each office and, while carrying the plotline of redemptive history, they typologically illustrated its fulfillment in the ministry of the coming Messiah, Jesus. Third, Jesus made a significant statement in John 14:12–14 to which we will inspect in greater detail below. For now, He told the church that we would continue the work that He had done

---

1. See, for example, the *Westminster Confession of Faith*, ch. 8; "Of Christ the Mediator;" the *Belgic Confession*, article 21; the *Heidelberg Catechism*, Q. 31 or the *Second Helvetic Confession*, XI.

*Theological Framework for the Prophet-Priest-King Paradigm*

and do greater works still. To understand this, we'll need to have understood the PPK framework in which He did His work.[2]

## TYPOLOGY: TYPE, ARCHETYPE, AND ECTYPE

R. T. France explains typology illustrates "the conviction of the unchanging principles of the working of God and of the continuity between his acts in the past and in the present."[3] That is, typology shows God's consistent dealings with men throughout redemptive history: His acts in the Old Testament established patterns that illustrated His acts in the New Testament. In fact, the continuity is so stable that Old Testament persons or events ("types") rightly understood in their context can be used to illustrate and understand persons or events ("anti-types") in the New Testament especially the ministry of the Lord Jesus. He explains, further:

> The idea of fulfilment inherent in the New Testament typology derives . . . from the conviction that in the coming and work of Jesus the principles of God's working, already imperfectly embodied in the Old Testament, were more perfectly re-embodied and thus brought to completion.[4]

In order to rightly identify types (versus allegories or predictive prophecies) there should be both historical and theological

---

2. It is very important to remember there are unique redemptive acts of the Lord Jesus that are not repeatable—acts that secured the salvation for all His people for all eternity. Neither Jesus nor the apostle John teaches the church will "do" these and "greater than these" will we do. Opponents of the PPK framework in the local church, like Timothy Paul Jones for example, point to these non-repeatable acts and claim the church cannot use such a framework because of them (Jones, "Prophets, Priests and Kings Today? Theological and Practical Problems with the Use of the Munus Triplex as a Leadership Typology," 63). However, as I will work to prove, in a way analogous to the work of the Holy Spirit completing what the Lord Jesus started (though it was finished [John 19:30]), what the church does is advance its mission of kingdom building according to the PPK framework in ways analogous to the ways the Old Testament prophets, priests, and kings did their work as well as to the way the Lord did His. In this way, the church does the works of Christ and greater works still.

3. France, *Jesus and the Old Testament*, 76.

4. France, *Jesus and the Old Testament*, 40.

correspondence between the Old Testament persons or events and those in the New Testament.⁵ This makes sense. The case of Jonah presents these clearly. Historically, Jonah's situation in the fish's belly presented an impossible problem that no skill or insight of man was able to solve. The same was true for Jesus' death: in His humanity, He could not escape death under the power of any wisdom or resolve of men. Both were solved by divine power: both men were "resurrected" from their deathly imprisonments. The theological correspondence was in their missions to be preachers of repentance to stiff-necked peoples. Both brought messages to the peoples in light of their miraculous resurrections.⁶ France explains there need not be correspondence in every detail but rather historical and theological patterns established in the Old Testament and repeated in the New indicates a type/anti-type relationship.⁷

It is this dynamic the church has used to explain the relationship between the men consecrated and ordained by God as prophets, priests, and kings in the Old Testament and the mediatorial roles of Christ in the New Testament. Jesus Himself saw and stepped into this dynamic.⁸ The common terminology to describe this framework is "type/anti-type."⁹ The "types" establish the patterns which the "anti-types" repeat and fulfill; the former historically add data to the event or person the latter gathers up and applies. In order to most clearly explain the main point of this chapter, we will use the more familiar "archetype" in place of the more specialized "anti-type."¹⁰

---

5. France, *Jesus and the Old Testament*, 41.

6. France, *Jesus and the Old Testament*, 44–45.

7. France, *Jesus and the Old Testament*, 41. Even Jesus makes this connection with Jonah: Matthew 12:38-41.

8. "It is to these [prophet, priest, and king] that Jesus looks for the 'pedigree' of his mediatorial work. In him, the three classes come together, and the types find their fulfillment." France, *Jesus and the Old Testament*, 49, 76.

9. Elwell and Beitzel, *Baker Encyclopedia of the Bible*, 2109–10. "Typology also explains how many of the events in Jesus' life and ministry are fulfilments of Old Testament patterns." Duane A. Garret, "Type, typology" in Elwell, *Evangelical Dictionary of Biblical Theology*, 785–87. See also Berkhof, *Systematic Theology*, 357.

10. "Archetype" is defined as "an original model or type after which other

*Theological Framework for the Prophet-Priest-King Paradigm*

## Type and Archetype

In the Old Testament, there are general types whose purpose is to display, witness, or example the archetype, the Lord Jesus, who is presented in the New Testament.[11] More importantly and specifically, the roles of the prophets, priests, and kings in Israel were types ultimately fulfilled by the Lord Jesus Christ, the archetype.[12]

It is true the Old Testament prophets, priests, and kings were not simply types of Christ; they were essential and truly advanced the will of God among the people of God. Yet each of them executed prophetic, priestly, and kingly ministries, ultimately as a means of God to illustrate some of the glories of the coming ministry of the Lord Jesus Christ. Whatever their roles in redemptive history, they should not be viewed apart from their contribution to revealing aspects of the beauty of the mediatorial work of the Lord. Charles Hodge summarizes:

> That this is not a merely figurative representation is plain from the fact that Christ exercised all the functions of a prophet, of a priest, and of a king. He was not simply so called, but the work which He actually performed included in perfection all that the ancient prophets, priests, and kings performed in a lower sphere and as an adumbration of Christ's more perfect work.[13]

---

similar things are patterned." *American Heritage Dictionary*, "Archetype."

11. These general types were found in such things as the bronze serpent on the pole (Num 21:9 // John 3:14), the Passover Lamb (Exod 12:43–49 // 1 Cor 5:7) or the water-giving rock (Exod 17:6 // 1 Cor 10:3–4).

12. For example, Moses, the "prophet" (Deut 34:10) was a type of the Lord Jesus as "final" Prophet (Heb 1:1–2). Moses predicted there would come "a prophet like me" (Deut 18:15) to lead Israel in the future. It was the apostle Peter, in his sermon in Acts 3:22 (cf. Acts 7:37), that confirmed the Lord Jesus was that prophet, the archetype to Moses, the type.

13. Hodge, *Systematic Theology*, 460.

Part Two | Typology Trajectory

## Archetype and Ectype

As we introduced above, the "types" found in the Old Testament find their fulfillment in Christ as the archetype. Each man who filled the roles of prophet, priest, or king, stood as an exemplar for the one who would come to sum up that aspect of the work as the Messiah.

With the Lord's advent and His finished work came the end of the role of "types." However, as the New Testament data demonstrates, the *finished* work of the Lord set the condition for the *finishing* work of the church. Importantly, in John 14, the Lord promised that those who believed in Him would do the works that He did and "greater works" than those even He did (John 14:12).[14] What can those who do such works in His name and on His behalf be called? An "ectype." An ectype is a reproduction or copy of an original.[15]

Building on the foundation of types and the archetype, the heart of this framework is that we can classify the prophetic, priestly, and kingly ministry of the New Testament church as ectypes empowered by the Holy Spirit to continue the ministry of the Lord Jesus in ways consistent with His own finished works. These New Testament ectypes, rather than pointing ahead to what the Lord Jesus Christ would fulfill, by the power of the Holy Spirit, apply in the church what the Lord has already accomplished.[16]

## THE OLD TESTAMENT TYPES

In order to understand the typological dynamic from type to ectype, we will consider the general categories of types and then

---

14. With the unfolding of the New Testament we see these works included some of the same kinds (e.g., miracles: Acts 8:13, 19:11) but also related or applicatory kinds of works (e.g., preaching: Acts 6:2). Those who did analogous works before Christ were called "types."

15. *American Heritage Dictionary*, "Ectype."

16. Letham, *Holy Trinity*, 47, 54–58. I can't stress this enough: the church is finishing what Christ has finished. As Paul states in Eph 2:20, we are building on what has been built and doing so in ways analogous to but not repeating the work of the builders.

how the Lord Jesus did His ministry as the archetype. In the next chapter, we'll begin to see how this lays the groundwork for the ministry of the church as ectypes.

## The Prophetical Office.

God had long declared His covenants with blessings and curses to His people directly. God spoke to Adam (Gen 3:15), to Noah (Gen 9:17), to Abraham (e.g., Gen 12:2, 15:1, 17:1–2, 22:15ff), to Isaac (Gen 26:2), and the descendants all the way to Moses. It was with Moses the Lord began to speak mediately to His people, that is, using him as a covenant spokesman instead of speaking directly to the people. God chose Moses to be the agent both declaring and bringing about the good news of Israel's redemption (Exod 3:10).

Afterward, Moses' role would be not just as God's deliverer of the people through their wilderness wandering, but also His prophet to them, e.g., "Tell all the congregation of Israel" (Exod 12:3). This is the functional equivalent of the later prophetic marker, "thus saith the Lord" (e.g., Isa 66:1) and would be the new norm for Moses. Not only was this the Lord's choice but, eventually, it was the people's:

> Now when all the people saw the thunder and the flashes of lightning and the sound of the trumpet and the mountain smoking, the people were afraid and trembled, and they stood far off and said to Moses, "You speak to us, and we will listen; but do not let God speak to us, lest we die."[17]

The formal announcement of the continuation of the prophetical office after Moses comes from Deut 18:15. Moses tells the people, "The LORD your God will raise up for you a prophet like me from among you, from your brothers—it is to him you shall listen." Moses spoke these words to his brethren after he warned them against joining in Canaanite worship in the Promised Land (Deut 18:9–12). He already knew he would not be joining the people as

---

17. Exod 20:18–19.

they crossed the Jordan (Deut 3:23–27) and with the warning not to consult diviners or fortune tellers, he assured them the Lord would raise up a prophet like him who will continue to declare the Lord's words as he had done.

The Lord affirmed what Moses had spoken to the people with the promise to him, "I will raise up for them a prophet like you from among their brothers. And I will put My words in his mouth, and he shall speak to them all that I command him" (Deut 18:17–18). In this short statement we see the two key parts of the prophet's ministry. First, the prophets will be anointed by God, that is He will give to them an endowment of power and authority from Himself to fulfill the charge, "I will put My words in his mouth."[18] Second, this anointing will sustain the prophet's task, "he shall speak to them all that I command him." Simply put, prophets speak of God for God.[19]

John Currid explains the fulfillment of this promise would be two-fold: God would establish the prophetic office in Israel to be filled by men (and women[20]) from Samuel through John the Baptist[21] and there would be future messianic fulfillment.[22] With the promise of messianic fulfilment we have the prophet's function as a "type." Perhaps the clearest biblical text carrying the typological messianic fulfilment motif to expression is found in Isaiah chapter 61:1–2.

> The Spirit of the Lord is upon me, because he has anointed me to proclaim good news to the poor. He has sent me

---

18. Calvin, *Institutes*, 495; Ursinus, *Commentary of Zacharias Ursinus on the Heidelberg Catechism*, 170; Brakel, *Christian's Reasonable Service*, 397.

19. Hodge, *Systematic Theology*, 462; Calvin, *Institutes*, 2.15.2, 496.

20. For example, Deborah (Judg 4:4) and Huldah (2 Kgs 22:14).

21. "This chapter ought, therefore, to be understood in such a sense, that Christ, who is the Head of the prophets, holds the chief place, and alone makes all those revelations; but that Isaiah, and the other prophets, and the apostles, contribute their services to Christ, and each performs his part in making known Christ's benefits." Calvin and Pringle, *Commentary on a Harmony of the Evangelists*, 2:303.

22. In support of the Messianic fulfillment, he cites John 6:14, 7:40. Currid, *Deuteronomy*, 322–23.

to proclaim liberty to the captives and recovering of sight to the blind, to set at liberty those who are oppressed, to proclaim the year of the Lord's favor.

Isaiah chapter 61 is an essential text in the last portion of Isaiah's prophecy, chapters 56–66.[23] John L. Mackay portrays its centrality in his "concentric analysis" of Isa 56–66, calling chapters 60–62 the center point in these last chapters.[24] Mackay points out these chapters recapitulate themes already found in Isaiah. These include, the sin-bearing Servant (chapter 53 // 60:10, 15), the expansion of the people of God (chapter 54 // 61:1–7), and the picture of the final victory of God (chapter 55 // 62:1–4). He explains, however, "the message of Scripture is not just about the existence of final glory. It is equally concerned with how one gets there."[25] In short, by the prophetic work (in this case) of the Messiah that is to come. Zion's redemption spoken of in Isaiah is the fruit of the work of the speaker in Isa 61:1–4. As Isaiah's prophecy makes clear, the one who will deliver the glad tidings to Zion will do so as Moses before Him: the Spirit-anointed proclaimer of God's word, that is, as a prophet of God.[26]

## The Priestly Office.

R. T. France comments, the priesthood "is the beginning of the typology which the Epistle to the Hebrews develops so fully, in which the Old Testament cultic institution and its officers are seen as 'symbolic for the present age,' 'a shadow of the good things to come.'"[27] Therefore, the starting point for a full understanding of the Lord as our priest begins in the two Old Testament priesthoods: of Melchizedek and of Aaron.

23. This section breakdown is highlighted in Webb, *Bible Speaks Today*. Motyer, *Isaiah*. Mackay, *Study Commentary on Isaiah*.

24. Mackay, *Isaiah*, 405; Motyer, *Isaiah*, 376.

25. Mackay, *Isaiah*, 407.

26. Mackay, *Isaiah*, 516–517. See also Elisha's call and commission in 1 Kgs 19:16, 2 Kgs 2:9.

27. France, *Jesus and the Old Testament*, 47.

## Part Two | Typology Trajectory

### *Melchizedek*

The priesthood of Melchizedek is introduced in the Bible first. Of Melchizedek, little is known. Genesis 14:18–20 gives us most of the biographical information provided:

> And Melchizedek king of Salem brought out bread and wine. (He was priest of God Most High.) And he blessed him and said, "Blessed be Abram by God Most High, Possessor of heaven and earth; and blessed be God Most High, who has delivered your enemies into your hand!" And Abram gave him a tenth of everything.

The context of this meeting was Abram's return from rescuing his nephew Lot who had been taken captive by Mesopotamian kings. From this text we learn several things. First, Melchizedek came out to greet Abram with bread and wine. It was Jonathan Edwards who commented, "The bread and wine signified the same blessings of the covenant of grace that the bread and wine do in the sacrament of the Lord's Supper."[28] Viewed in this way it seems Melchizedek was some kind of authorized representative of the covenant of grace. Given to Abram by God in Gen 12 (expanded in chapters 15 and 17), perhaps in this act of Melchizedek's generosity, he was portraying the signs and seals of the covenant to Abram. It is likely we can draw a line from this act of Melchizedek to the Lord's actions in the Lord's Supper with the disciples (e.g., Matthew 26:26–29).

Second, Melchizedek was king of "Salem." Based on its use in Ps 76, "Salem" is thought to be a shortened form of Jerusalem. Psalm 76:1–3:

> In Judah God is known; his name is great in Israel. His abode has been established in Salem, his dwelling place in Zion. There he broke the flashing arrows, the shield, the sword, and the weapons of war.

---

28. "History of the Work of Redemption," in Edwards, *Works of Jonathan Edwards*, 1:544.

## Theological Framework for the Prophet-Priest-King Paradigm

Jerusalem was the place where God put His name (Ps 76:1). It was where the temples of God were built and rebuilt and the priesthood of Aaron served the Lord. It is where Israel's king ruled and reigned. It is the place where the throne of David's prophesied successor would sit (2 Sam 7:14; Isa 9:7). It was the place where the last sacrifice was made (Matt 27:50). In Israel's history, the connections with Jerusalem could not be overstated, and in Melchizedek and his blessing of Abram, these are depicted in type-form.

Melchizedek was also a priest of God Most High, "El Elyon." This is the first instance in the Bible where the word "priest" is used, though no other descriptions of the priesthood ministry are given beyond the priestly blessing upon Abram. And the title "God Most High" is only used here and in Ps 57 as a designation for YHWH, the God of Israel.[29] In his position, Melchizedek was authorized to bless others as a representative of God as well as offer Him pleasing worship as he "blessed God Most High."[30] Abram's response to the priest-king was to honor him with a tithe of all he recovered in his efforts to save Lot. This act of voluntary respect and veneration for Melchizedek typologically grounds giving worship to the great high priest of the new covenant, Jesus Christ (e.g., 2 Cor 9:6–8).

Finally, from Heb 7:3 we have additional biographical information pertinent to our topic: "[Melchizedek] is without father or mother or genealogy, having neither beginning of days nor end of life, but resembling the Son of God he continues a priest forever." These statements by the writer of Hebrews aren't meant to indicate Melchizedek wasn't a man with a father, mother, birthday or death. Rather, as the first of the Lord's priesthood, he was "a perfect type of the Lord Jesus."[31]

---

29. Ps 57:2. Additionally, in Gen 14:22, in speaking to the king of Sodom, Abram indicates Yahweh whom he serves and "God Most High" are equivalent. The Hebrew words in both places are the same.

30. "Amid the corruptions of the world, he alone, in that land, was an upright and sincere cultivator and guardian of religion." Calvin, *Genesis*, 388.

31. Pink, *Gleanings in Genesis*, 160.

Part Two | Typology Trajectory

Melchizedek is not mentioned again until Ps 110. There, in the royal, messianic psalm,[32] we discover his priesthood was later given special designation, "The Lord has sworn and will not change his mind, 'You are a priest forever after the order of Melchizedek.'" Of this psalm, M. J. Paul explains, "It is appreciated to such a degree by the NT authors, that it is the one quoted most of all. Especially in the Epistle to the Hebrews it is used to work out the concept that Christ is a priest after the order of Melchizedek."[33] No one is designated in this priesthood apart from the Lord Jesus. Outside of Gen 14 and Ps 110, Melchizedek is mentioned only in Heb 5–7.[34] In summary, his priestly order is given special designation because it was a type of the priesthood the Lord would fill: unrelated to the Aaronic priesthood, unending, worthy of veneration and worship.

*Aaron*

The priesthood of Aaron came much later in the history of redemption. In Exod 28:1, the Lord instructed Moses to bring his brother, Aaron, and his sons forward to be priests. In the administration of the covenant of grace, the Lord chose to use Moses and his brother Aaron to save the people from their captivity in Egypt and make a way for their regular worship in sacrifice at the tabernacle through the mediation of anointed priests.

Whereas the ministry of Melchizedek was limited to his serving Abram the emblems of the covenant of grace and blessing him, Zacharias Ursinus describes the expanded ministry of the Aaronic priesthood as those who are "appointed of God, for the purpose of offering oblations and sacrifices, for interceding, and teaching others."[35]

---

32. Kidner, *Psalms* 73–150, 391–92. Gaebelein et al., *Expositor's Bible Commentary*, 696.

33. Paul, "Order of Melchizedek (Ps 110:4 and Heb 7:3)," 195.

34. Heb 5:6, 10; 6:20; 7:1, 10, 11, 15, 17.

35. Ursinus, *Commentary*, 174; Beeke and Smalley, *Reformed Systematic Theology*, 992.

### Theological Framework for the Prophet-Priest-King Paradigm

In the Aaronic priesthood, combined with the Melchizedekian one, we have the essential functions of the priest: blessing, teaching the law, offering sacrifices, and intercessory prayer. These duties of the priests are explained in the book of Leviticus. Their duties concerning sacrifice were written in chapter 4 (see Exod 29:38–42), concerning intercession in chapter 16 (and Num 6:23–26) and concerning instruction in chapter 10. Additionally, in chapters 21–22, they were commanded in numerous ways to lives of holiness. Leviticus 21 provides a summary:

> ⁶They shall be holy to their God and not profane the name of their God. For they offer the Lord's food offerings, the bread of their God; therefore they shall be holy . . . . ⁸You shall sanctify him, for he offers the bread of your God. He shall be holy to you, for I, the Lord, who sanctify you, am holy.

### The Kingly Office.

God's people have always had a king.[36] In the most general terms, the kingly office is one of rule, power, and defense.[37] In the history of God's people, God's role as our king has been illustrated repeatedly.[38] Though He had not spoken of Himself as king until the time of the prophet Samuel, He had overseen His people as their king. Moses predicted the people would one day reject the Lord as their king and ask for a human king (Deut 17:14–15). In fact, when the people became dissatisfied with the sons of Samuel and their corrupt judgments, requesting a king, Samuel had this exchange with the Lord (1 Sam 8:6–8):

> And Samuel prayed to the Lord. And the Lord said to Samuel, "Obey the voice of the people in all that they say to you, for they have not rejected you, but they have

---

36. Beeke and Smalley, *Reformed Systematic Theology*, 1113.

37. Ursinus, *Commentary*, 176; Beeke and Smalley, *Reformed Systematic Theology*, 1117.

38. For example, Deut 33:5. Even Balaam recognized it: Num 23:21.

rejected me from being king over them. According to all the deeds that they have done, from the day I brought them up out of Egypt even to this day, forsaking me and serving other gods, so they are also doing to you."

However, far more than a concession because of their sinfulness, the Lord's choice of men to be kings over His people was an intentional covenantal act. As Adam before them, these kings would rule as vice-regents of the Lord in Israel. Through these men, the Lord would continue to keep His covenantal promises to Adam and Abraham. First, Saul (1 Sam 10:1) and then David after him (1 Sam 16:1, 12–13) became princes over the people. Saul was eventually rejected by the Lord for his persistent disobedience (1 Sam 15:11, 22–23). David, however, was intended for better things by the Lord, namely, to be a type of the Messiah who was to come.[39]

It was written of David, he "knew that the LORD had established him king over Israel, and that He had exalted his kingdom for the sake of His people Israel" (2 Sam 5:12). Shortly after the return of the ark of the covenant to Jerusalem, David was moved to build the Lord a house, a temple. The prophet Nathan encouraged him to do so until the Lord appeared to Nathan in a dream. In that dream, he was told to speak to David concerning his intentions:

> When your days are fulfilled and you lie down with your fathers, I will raise up your offspring after you, who shall come from your body, and I will establish his kingdom. He shall build a house for my name, and I will establish the throne of his kingdom forever. I will be to him a father, and he shall be to me a son. When he commits iniquity, I will discipline him with the rod of men, with the stripes of the sons of men, but my steadfast love will not depart from him, as I took it from Saul, whom I put away from before you. And your house and your kingdom shall be made sure forever before me. Your throne shall be established forever.

Here, in 2 Sam 7:12–16, the Lord made a covenant with David concerning David's line firmly establishing King David as a type of

---

39. France, *Jesus and the Old Testament*, 47.

## Theological Framework for the Prophet-Priest-King Paradigm

Christ. Its importance is amplified in Isa 9:1–7, especially verse 7: "Of the increase of his government and of peace there will be no end, on the throne of David and over his kingdom, to establish it and to uphold it with justice and with righteousness from this time forth and forevermore. The zeal of the Lord of hosts will do this." The throne of David will be established in steadfast love and faithfulness (Isa 16:5, 55:3). Jeremiah also speaks of the coming king, a "Righteous Branch" of David who will save Israel and Judah and be called "the Lord is our righteousness" (Jer 23:5–6). The prophet Ezekiel (34:23–24) speaks of this king as a shepherd: "And I will set up over them one shepherd, my servant David, and he shall feed them: he shall feed them and be their shepherd. And I, the LORD, will be their God, and my servant David shall be prince among them. I am the LORD; I have spoken."

Finally, the true significance of the covenant the Lord made with David, seen in the prophecies above, was in his archetype, the Lord Jesus. Robert Bergen notes,

> The significance of the eternal covenant between the Lord and David for the New Testament writers cannot be overemphasized. These words played an essential preparatory role in developing the messianic expectations that were fulfilled in Jesus. The hopes that were raised by the Lord's words—that God would place a seed of David on an eternal throne and establish a kingdom that would never perish—were ones that no Israelite or Judahite monarch satisfied, or even could have satisfied. But they were ones that the first-century Christians understood Jesus to fulfill.[40]

In the next chapter, we will look at the work of the Lord Jesus in the three offices of prophet, priest, and king according to the Scriptures. Once again, this is the necessary next step in understanding how the PPK paradigm unites and oversees local church ministry.

---

40. Bergen, *1, 2 Samuel*, 337.

# CHAPTER THREE

## Jesus the Messiah: Archetype Prophet, Priest, and King

THE WESTMINSTER LARGER CATECHISM (*WLC*) answers this question: "Who is the Mediator of the covenant of grace?"

> The only Mediator of the covenant of grace is the Lord Jesus Christ, who, being the eternal Son of God, of one substance and equal with the Father, in the fullness of time became man, and so was and continues to be God and man, in two entire distinct natures and one person, forever.[1]

The catechism further connects the mediator of the new covenant with the three offices needed to execute His mediatorship: of a prophet, of a priest, and of a king. It answers the question, "Why was our Mediator called Christ?"

> Our Mediator was called Christ because he was anointed with the Holy Ghost above measure; and so set apart, and fully furnished with all authority and ability, to execute the offices of prophet, priest and king of his church, in the estate both of his humiliation and exaltation.[2]

---

1. Presbyterian Church in America, *Westminster Confession of Faith*, 179.
2. *WLC*, Q.42.

### Jesus the Messiah: Archetype Prophet, Priest, and King

John Calvin, in his 1559 edition of the *Institutes of the Christian Religion*, is credited for bringing the PPK into regular usage among Reformed theologians.³ In fact, by the mid-nineteenth century, Charles Hodge explained the usage of the PPK to describe the mediatorial work of the Lord Jesus had long been customary and was of "substantive importance and has a firm Scriptural basis."⁴ He also wrote of the necessity of Christ in these offices: "We, as fallen men, ignorant, guilty, polluted and helpless, need a Saviour who is a prophet to instruct us; a priest to atone and to make intercession for us; and a king to rule over and protect us."⁵

Reformed theologians since Calvin have connected the PPK with the mediatorial work of Christ; it is how the Reformed have come to understand the Lord's work. In fact, God prepared His people to receive the work of the Messiah by ordaining and anointing men in the Old Testament who would serve as prophets, priests, and kings.

In order to better understand how the church conducts its work according to the PPK paradigm, we will consider in some depth key New Testament passages that assign Jesus as the Archetype to which the types point.

## SECTION 1: JESUS AS THE FINAL PROPHET

Introduction: Luke 4:16–21.

A key New Testament passage is Luke 4:16–21. At this point in Luke's gospel, the Lord Jesus has returned to the region of Galilee subsequent to His temptation trial in the desert and has begun His public ministry. The Spirit's power was plainly and remarkably evident in the Lord as He was already making a significant impact and His fame spread, "a report about Him went out through all the surrounding country" (Luke 4:14). Luke tells us the first activity

---

3. Vos, *Reformed Dogmatics*, 87.
4. Hodge, *Systematic Theology*, 459.
5. Hodge, *Systematic Theology*, 461; Geerhardus Vos asserts that only those who embrace this have the "whole" Christ, *Reformed Dogmatics*, 88.

of the Lord, in the power of the Holy Spirit, was that He "taught in their synagogues" (Luke 4:15). Luke 4:16–21 may be translated according to Figure 1 below.[6]

| Verse | Line | |
|---|---|---|
| 16 | 1 | And He came to Nazareth |
|  | 2 | where He had been raised |
|  | 3 | And He came into |
|  | 4 | (according to His customary practice on the Sabbath day) |
|  | 5 | to the synagogue and |
|  | 6 | He stood to read aloud. |
| 17 | 7 | The scroll of the prophet Isaiah was given to Him |
|  | 8 | And, unrolling the scroll, He found the place where it was written: |
| 18 | 9 | The Spirit of the Lord is upon Me |
|  | 10 | because He has anointed Me |
|  | 11 | to proclaim good news to the poor |
|  | 12 | He has sent Me |
|  | 13 | to preach freedom to the captives |
|  | 14 | and recovery of sight to the blind |
|  | 15 | to send out the ones being oppressed in freedom |
| 19 | 16 | to preach the year of favor of the Lord. |
| 20 | 17 | And rolling up the scroll, giving it to the officer, |
|  | 18 | He sat. |
|  | 19 | And all the eyes in the synagogue were fixed on Him. |
| 21 | 20 | He began to say, "Today, this Scripture has been fulfilled in your hearing." |

**Figure 1.**

## Commentary.

Luke gives a detailed account of the long-awaited public preaching ministry of the Lord.[7] In fact, Joel Green explains the larger passage

---

6. This and all subsequent translations are mine.
7. Bock, *Luke* 1:1–9:50, 402.

## Jesus the Messiah: Archetype Prophet, Priest, and King

this text begins (4:14–9:50), "Demonstrates how Jesus, empowered by the Spirit, understood the nature of his vocation and engaged in its performance by means of an itinerant ministry balancing proclamation and miraculous activity." We see three things in verses 16–20: the heart of the Lord's message, His typical target audience, and a paradigmatic response. In other words, here we read what is likely a typical example of Jesus' itinerant prophetic ministry.[8]

*Lines 1–2 (v. 16). "And He came to Nazareth where He had been raised."*

In verses 14–15 Luke narrates Jesus' return from the desert. Beginning in verse 16, Luke gets site-and-event specific[9] placing this scene at the beginning of the Lord's ministry in order to illustrate it.[10] Luke explains the Lord came back to Nazareth, "where He had been raised." Nazareth is in the region of Galilee so it follows from verse 14.

*Lines 3–6 (v.16). ". . . and He came into (according to His customary practice on the Sabbath day) to the synagogue and He stood to read aloud."*

"Customary practice" means "to continue to carry out a custom or tradition."[11] This is just what Jesus did: He did it with His parents

---

8. Green, *The Gospel of Luke*, 207.

9. The placement of this event here differs with the parallel passages in Matthew (13:53–58) and Mark (6:1–6). In Matthew and Mark, the event appears to have happened at a significantly later stage in Jesus' ministry. However, though Luke's placement serves a theological purpose (rather than a chronological one), it is likely the same event. Geldenhuys, *Gospel of Luke*, 167.; Marshall, *Gospel of Luke*, 177.

10. Marshall believes it is possible Luke brought this story to the beginning of the Lord's ministry to illustrate consistent motifs of His ministry including Spirit-empowered teaching as well as hard-hearted rejection. Marshall, *Gospel of Luke*, 177–178. See also Green, *Gospel of Luke*, 207.

11. Louw and Nida, *Greek-English Lexicon*, 506. Luke 2:27, "And [Simeon] came in the Spirit into the temple and when the parents brought in the child

Part Two | Typology Trajectory

as a boy, and it is His customary practice. Luke portrays Jesus as an historically pious, regularly observant Jew.[12] The exact order of service in the synagogue is not known.[13] The generally agreed elements included: (a) prayer, (b) readings of Hebrew scriptures (Torah and Prophets), (c) paraphrasing into Aramaic, and (d) an invitation for someone to instruct the audience.[14] Jesus' fame, widespread acceptance, and "hometown" status must have earned Him the opportunity to lead in a portion of the service.[15]

*Lines 7-8 (v. 17). "The scroll of the prophet Isaiah was given to Him. And, unrolling the scroll, He found the place where it was written . . .*

At the appropriate time in the service, He stood to read aloud. It was customary to stand to read the Scriptures just as it was customary to sit to present instruction.[16] Verse 17 reads, "The scroll of the prophet Isaiah was given to Him and, unrolling the scroll, He found the place where it was written . . ." This translation is preferred as codices were not in use in the Christian church at this time.[17] Synagogues were unevenly equipped with scrolls of Old Testament books. A specific synagogue had on hand what it could afford.[18] Luke does not make it clear why the scroll of Isaiah was selected

---

Jesus to do for Him according to the custom of the Law. . ."

12. Geldenhuys, *Luke*, 167.

13. Marshall suggest this is the oldest known account of a synagogue service, *Luke*, 181. See also Stein, *Luke*, 155. Different commentaries make different suggestions on the order of service: Bock, *Luke 1:1–9:50*, 403; Green, *Gospel of Luke*, 209, Geldenhuys, *Luke*, 167; Osborne, *Luke*, 115–16.

14. Bock, *Luke*, 403; Geldenhuys, *Luke*, 167; Marshall, *Luke*, 181; Osborne, *Luke*, 115–116; Stein, *Luke*, 155.

15. Geldenhuys, *Luke*, 167.

16. Bock, *Luke*, 403.

17. Stein comments, "Some manuscripts (A,B,L,W) read 'opened' perhaps because the word used for scroll here is *biblion*, which later came to mean a *codex* or *book*. 'Unrolling,' however, is the better reading and a more appropriate expression for the opening of a scroll." Stein, *Luke*, 155.

18. Osborne, *Luke*, 116.

and given to the Lord.[19] However, in light of his use of "he found," the Lord intentionally made His way through the scroll until He found the exact stopping place. Marshall writes, "The suggestion that the scroll opened by chance at the appropriate place is alien to the sense of [found] and to the stress on the initiative of Jesus."[20]

*Lines 9 (v.18). "The Spirit of the Lord is upon Me..."*

Providentially, this is not surprising. Luke had already written of the Spirit's descent upon the Lord anointing and ordaining Him to His mediatorial work (3:21–22; cf. 1:35, 2:25). Likewise, the Spirit's presence in Jesus' ministry is before (4:1) and after His desert temptation-trial (4:14). Luke's citation is a slightly adapted version of Isaiah 61:1–2 and 58:6 from the Septuagint (LXX), the Greek translation of the Old Testament. This latter part of Isaiah is concerned about Zion's deliverance. Beale and Carson highlight in Isaiah chs. 60–62 that deliverance is by a single individual with the special anointing of the Spirit.[21] Ridderbos writes, "The appearance of the messenger of joyful news in 61:1ff. (*cf.* 40:9; 41:27; 52:7) becomes the programme [sic] of Jesus' ministry in Lk. 4:17ff."[22] The prophetic ministry of the Lord anticipated here in Isa 61 and 58 is the declaration of the reversal of fortunes of God's oppressed people.

---

19. Marshall believes He requested it (*Luke*, 182).

20. Marshall, *Luke*, 182, italics in original.

21. Beale and Carson, *Commentary on the New Testament Use of the Old Testament*, 288. They note the Targum affirmed the prophetic nature of the text explicitly identifying the speaker as the Prophet.

22. N. H. Ridderbos, "Isaiah, Book Of," ed. Wood et al., *New Bible Dictionary*, 513.

*Lines 10–15 (v.18). "... because He has anointed Me to proclaim the good news to the poor, He has sent me to preach freedom to the captives and recovery of sight to the blind, to send out the ones being oppressed in freedom ...*

The reversal motif is at the heart of Luke 4:18–19; it defines the prophet's ministry. Two main verbs govern the four related actions of the Messiah. In both cases the subject is the Holy Spirit and the object is the Lord Jesus. The first is "He anointed," and the second is "He has sent."

"He anointed" grammatically oversees the following action, "to proclaim the good news." This answers the question, "For what purpose does the Spirit anoint?" The Spirit's anointing is for the ministry of the prophetic proclamation. This ministry will be focused on the "poor." BAGD defines the "poor" in this context as referring "not only to the unfavorable circumstances of these people from an economic point of view; the thought is also that since they are oppressed and disillusioned they are in special need of God's help."[23] In this way, "He anointed Me to proclaim good news to the poor" becomes the overall heading as well as summary of the prophetic ministry of the Lord.[24]

We might expect the follow-on three verbs found in verses 18 and 19 ("to preach," "to send," and "to preach") to be stacked on top of one another more fully extending "to proclaim the good news." Instead, these explain the intent behind the second governing verb, "He has sent." The question these verbs answer is, "What is the Sent One to do?" He is "to preach," "to send out," and "to preach." Let's consider them in turn.

First, He is sent "to preach freedom to the captives and recovery of sight to the blind." The message of the Prophet, the good news, is "liberty" to the captives. Since "poor" is understood as

---

23. *BAGD*, 728. Bock calls this designation a, "soteriological generalization" meaning those to whom the preaching is delivered and describe who accept it, Bock, *Luke*, 408.

24. Luke's omission of the next part of Isa 61:1, "to bind up the brokenhearted" (though true, e.g., 7:11–15) is meant to tightly focus Jesus' point: what is preeminent for the Lord is His prophetic ministry (cf. Mark 1:15).

## Jesus the Messiah: Archetype Prophet, Priest, and King

a larger-than-economic category, "captives" may be something larger than simple physical imprisonment. We can also follow major translations of the word "liberty" (here) and "forgiveness" elsewhere (Luke 1:77, 3:3, 24:47), as freedom from sin and spiritual captivity. Interestingly, this word dominates the LXX discussion of the "Year of Jubilee" in Lev 25.[25] In addition, the preaching of the Prophet includes, to the blind, the "recovery of sight," that is freedom of a different kind. These words "blind" and "recovery of sight" have both literal, physical meanings but also spiritual and metaphorical ones.[26] As with "liberty" one can envision the Prophet declaring something tangible and experiential (e.g., regained eyesight, e.g., 18:35-43) and also something spiritual and eternal (e.g., healthy eye filled with spiritual light, e.g., 11:33-36).

Second, the Prophet was sent in order "to send out, in liberty, the ones being oppressed." This is not found in the LXX of Isaiah 61:1. Rather, it comes from Isa 58:6. Of Isa 58:6, the ESV reads, "Is not this the fast that I choose: . . . to let the oppressed go free." The LXX reads more actively and strongly, " 'I have not chosen such a fast as this,' says the Lord. Instead . . . send the broken ones forth in forgiveness."

Two notes are required. First, in the LXX, the verb "send" is an active command.[27] This supports my translation of Luke 4:18 as "to send out" (vs. ESV, "set at"). In Isa 58, God commands the "broken ones" be sent forth in "forgiveness." While in Isaiah the agent is generally God (e.g. 58:9), Jesus incorporates this into the ministry of the eschatological Prophet by grouping it in with Isa 61. Second, "the ones being oppressed" translates the fact that

---

25. Lev 25:10, 11, 12, 13, 28, 30, 31, 33, 40, 50, 52, 54.

26. Bock, *Luke*, 409; Marshall writes, "Recovery of sight is in the Lukan narrative clearly an issue of physical healing (cf. 18:35-43; Acts 9:18-19) but it is also presented as a metaphor for receiving revelation and experiencing salvation and inclusion in God's family (see already 1:78-79; 2:9, 29-32; 3:6), *Luke*, 211. Stein concurs, "There is another sense, however, in which 'blind' refers metaphorically to those who are "spiritually blind." Stein, *Luke*, 156.

27. This present imperative carries forward the sense of the Hebrew verb, which is a Piel infinitive construct, that is, an intensified present tense form of the Qal. Futato, *Beginning Biblical Hebrew*, 175.

## Part Two | Typology Trajectory

their oppression has endured to this day. Neither Isaiah nor Luke give explicit detail on the nature of the oppression or brokenness. However, as with the terms "liberty," "captives," or "blind," we can broaden our understanding of the Lord's intent to include those physically oppressed (e.g., 4:31–36) and those oppressed by their sins (e.g., 5:20). Taken together, this is more than a simple prophetic message. Bock comments, "While a prophet could proclaim the message of liberty for the oppressed, he could not bring it to pass."[28] The Lord's insertion of Isa 58 was intended to present His prophetic ministry as more than messages from God, but also the actions of God (cf. John 6:38).[29]

Third, the prophet was sent "to preach the year of the Lord's favor." If verse 18 offered a heading for the ministry of the prophet, then this would be a fitting summary. This brings together the concepts of the "poor," the "captives," and the "ones being oppressed" with encouraging statements of "liberty" and the "recovery of sight." Likewise, the use of "liberty" here and in Lev 25 give this "year of the Lord's favor" an eschatological jubilee sense.

Overall, such actions by the prophet would certainly represent the favor of the Lord. A "year" of favor as opposed to a moment or an event of favor signals a significant change. "Year" is not likely to be considered a calendar year marked by (at the time) the phases of the next twelve moons. Rather, the jubilee concepts such as freeing of slaves, cancellation of debts, resting land and the return of property to family ownership signaled a fresh start for the people. Osborne believes, "Christ means that 'the year of the Lord's favor' has come with the dawn of the messianic age, the coming of salvation and of the Holy Spirit."[30]

---

28. Bock, *Luke*, 409.

29. This "extension" is an example of how the Lord's archetype ministry not only gathered but also extended the ministry of types before Him.

30. Osborne, *Luke*, 117.

*Jesus the Messiah: Archetype Prophet, Priest, and King*

***Lines 17-19 (v.20). "And rolling up the scroll, giving it to the officer, He sat. And all the eyes in the synagogue were fixed on Him."***

Luke slow-walks the scene to build anticipation in the reader. Having stood to receive it and read, He then sat to teach from it.[31] The forward placement of "all" in this phrase indicates a heightened expectation that Jesus would say something. Luke's prose is gripping, literally, "all the eyes in the synagogue were fixed on Him."

***Line 20 (v.21). "He began to say, 'Today, this Scripture has been fulfilled in your hearing.'"***

The verb set, "He began to say" should be taken as the opening remarks in a larger discourse.[32] In other words, He began with these words and continued to teach to them such that, in the end, "All spoke well of Him and marveled at the gracious words that were coming from His mouth" (4:22). While it is probably not appropriate to think of the "year of the Lord's favor" as only a year, Jesus' use of "Today" might best be understood as the actual day the fulfillment of Isaiah's prophecy was inaugurated, i.e., the first day of the era of the Lord's favor. "Today" "is a key term in Luke's theology and stresses that the opportunity for salvation is this very moment."[33] The fulfillment has begun.

## Conclusion.

Westminster Larger Catechism, Q. 43 asks, "How does Christ execute the office of a prophet?" The answer is, "Christ executes the office of a prophet, in His revealing to the Church, in all ages, by His

---

31. For example Bock, *Luke*, 399; Green, *Luke*, 209. Marshall highlights Jesus' posture, sitting to teach vs. just resuming His place, Marshall, *Luke*, 184; see also Geldenhuys, *Luke*, 167.

32. Marshall, *Luke*, 184–185; Geldenhuys, *Luke*, 168.

33. Bock, *Luke*, 412.

Spirit and Word, in diverse ways of administration, the whole will of God in all things concerning their edification and salvation."[34]

The Lord's use of Isa 61 and His opening statements in teaching it to the synagogue prove He is the final prophet. Prophets are ordained by God to speak of God for God. Luke has already recorded the anointing of the Lord (3:21–22) as well as the Spirit abiding presence with Him (4:1,14). What remained was to observe His message. Stepping into the shoes of eschatological prophet of Isa 61 with the gospel message of liberty, sight and salvation clearly put Him in the company of the old covenant prophets whose messages were previews to His own. The subtle inclusion of Isa 58:6 added a powerful fulfillment element to the proclamation.

## SECTION 2: JESUS AS THE FINAL HIGH PRIEST

Introduction.

Having taken on human flesh as our final high priest, He offered Himself as sacrifice for justice and reconciliation, and He intercedes for us. With Heb 5:1 as the background, Geerhardus Vos explains, "the work of a high priest is not so much to represent God before men as it is to represent men before God."[35] As priests they were (1) appointed men, who were (2) sacrifice-overseers securing covenant relationship to God,[36] and (3) intercessors seeking the grace of the covenant for the people.[37]

The book of Hebrews answers the question, "How can we approach God?"[38] It provides the answer in the "singular and matchless presentation of our Lord Jesus Christ."[39] Christ is "the essential and inseparable culmination of God's purpose for his one people

---

34. Beeke and Ferguson, *Reformed Confessions*, 69.
35. Vos, *Reformed Dogmatics*, 3:94.
36. E.g., Aaron: Lev 4, 9:22–23
37. E.g., Melchizedek: Gen 14:19; Aaron: Lev 16
38. Guthrie, *Hebrews*, 15–16.
39. Phillips, *Hebrews*, xv.

under old and new dispensations alike."[40] In order to see the role of the Lord Jesus as our final high priest, we turn to several passages in Hebrews. Its overall structure for our purposes is found in Figure 1. The passages that are directly relevant to our focus on Jesus as the high priest are in boldface type.

| | | | |
|---|---|---|---|
| **2:14–18** | **One like us to be our priest** | | |
| | 3:1–2, 5–6 | Jesus who was faithful | 3:6b: Let us hold fast our confidence |
| | | | 3:12–13: Let us exhort one another |
| | 4:9–11 | One to pass through death to carry us to our rest | |
| | 4:14 | Jesus who passed | 4:14 Let us hold fast |
| | 4:15 | One to hold fast for us | |
| | | Jesus tempted as we are | |
| | | | 4:16 Let us draw near to receive help and mercy |
| | 5:5–6 | One appointed Melchizedekian priest | |
| | 5:9–10 | He is the source of our eternal salvation | |
| | 6:19–20 | Christ is the fulfilled oath of God giving us access behind Him | |
| | 7:20–24 | Whose term won't end | |
| **7:23–25** | **One who intercedes** | | |
| | 7:26–27 | Unhindered by His sins | |
| **9:11–14** | **One sacrifice to guarantee our standing** | | |
| | 10:12–14 | One to finish the work | |
| | | | 10:22—Let us draw near |
| | | | 12:12—Let us not become wearied in our work |

**Figure 1.**

---

40. Ellingworth, *Epistle to the Hebrews*, 80.

Part Two | Typology Trajectory

## Commentary.

Our task is to present scriptural proof that the Lord Jesus was the archetype priest standing in line of the types of priests of the Old Testament. In those three boldface passages, we will shorten our study of them by looking at the overall argument of each, consider its keywords contributing to that sense, and then offer a summary conclusion.

Main text A. "One like us to be our priest," Heb 2:14–18.

The first critical part of priestly ministry is advocacy for fellow brethren as one of many appointed to the role of priest. A translation of the passage is in Figure 2.

> ¹⁴As, therefore, the children have a share in blood and flesh, He also, in like manner partook of them that through the death He might destroy the one who has the power of death, that is, the devil ¹⁵and pay for those who, out of fear of death, have always lived as subjects to slavery. ¹⁶For surely it is not angels that He helps but the offspring of Abraham He helps. ¹⁷Therefore, it was necessary that, according to every likeness of the brothers, He be made like them so that He might be a merciful and faithful high priest in God's service to be making conciliation for the sins of the people. ¹⁸For because He Himself had suffered when tempted, He is able to come to the aid of those being tempted.

Figure 2.

## *The Argument.*

The children (of Abraham) are of blood and flesh, and the Lord partook of the same that He might both destroy the devil's power over the same and pay for those who have been enslaved to him.[41] He doesn't do this for angels but for Abraham's offspring. In taking

---

41. Bruce, *Hebrews*, 84; Owen, *Epistle to the Hebrews*, 31.

on blood and flesh, He was appropriately like them to be both payment for their sins and their needed high priest before God.[42] To be like them, suffering in like manner, He is able to come to their aid.

## Key words.

The overall concept in this passage is the Lord taking on the human likeness of His people. "The children" in this passage are the "brothers" (2:11,12), the ones "God has given Me" (2:13) as well as the "offspring of Abraham" (2:16). Though what the Lord assumed in human flesh is common to all men, this last designation narrows its redemptive impact down to those who share Abraham's faith heritage, the line of promise. They "have a share" in blood and flesh, namely, it is who they are: human.

The author states the obvious in a way that is significant for making the point the Lord Jesus took on like human flesh.[43] He participated ("has a share") in humanity because of taking on human blood and flesh.[44] Ellingworth summarizes it, "The children share permanently with one another a common human nature and at a particular time Jesus himself also shared it with them."[45] The Lord did this so that by His substitutionary death He might destroy[46] the power the devil currently has over the children.[47]

---

42. Ellingworth, *Hebrews*, 170.
43. Bauer and Gingrich, *Greek-English Lexicon*, 514.
44. The apostle Paul uses this concept to explain the sealing action of the Lord's Supper in 1 Cor 10:16–17. When God's people eat, the elect are participating in Christ in ways analogous to how the Hebrews writer says Christ participates in human blood and flesh.
45. Ellingworth, *Hebrews*, 171.
46. *BAGD*, 416.
47. "The one who has power over death is himself reduced to impotence." Ellingworth, *Hebrews*, 173.

## Part Two | Typology Trajectory

As a partaker of blood and flesh, His death paid[48] the debt of enslavement to the tyrannous fear of death.[49] That payment was propitiatory. None of this would've been possible apart from the Lord taking to Himself human flesh and the helping[50] in human obligations (rather than angelic ones). The author returns to the importance of the Lord being made in every respect the likeness[51] of the brothers in ways appropriate to His nature, that is, neither fully putting down His deity (Phil. 2:5–8) nor assuming the fallenness of humanity (cf. 4:15). He takes blood and flesh, a "likeness" of us that is real but appropriate to Him doing so as God.[52]

At this point in the argument, the Lord in our likeness is not for the purpose of destroying the devil's power (cf. 2:14; 1 John 3:8) by paying the ransom price for release from slavery but rather for the merciful and faithful high priestly[53] service in the concerns of God. Of course, these are related in the priesthood of Aaron but are combined together in Christ as sacrifice (see below) as well as officiant (here).[54]

His merciful and faithful service is for the purpose of making conciliation[55] for the sins of the people. *BAGD* gives two related definitions of this word as (1) "propitiate, conciliate" and (2) "expiate" choosing "expiate" in the case of this verse.[56] David Allen ex-

---

48. "Free, release" with transitive verbs, *BAGD*, 80; Ellingworth, *Hebrews*, 174.

49. Bruce, *Hebrews*, 86; Guthrie, *Hebrews*, 93.

50. Ellingworth, *Hebrews*, 176. Bruce highlights the use of this term in 8:9 where God took hold of Israel to bring them out of Egypt, *Hebrews*, 87.

51. *BAGD*, 567.

52. Owen says, "He was made like unto His brethren in the essence of human nature—a rational, spiritual soul and a mortal body quickened by its union therewithal." Owen, *Hebrews*, 35.

53. I take these two words to modify "high priest." See for example, Ellingworth, *Hebrews*, 181; Guthrie, *Hebrews*, 94; Calvin, *Hebrews*, 73.

54. Referring to the Lord as high priest is common in Hebrews: 3:1; 4:14f; 5:5–10; 6:20; 7:26; 8:1; 9:1.

55. ESV cites this text and Luke 18:13 as the two occurrences in the New Testament. A related word, "mercy seat," is in 9:5.

56. *BAGD*, 375; as does Ellingworth cautiously, *Hebrews*, 189.

plains, "The difference between 'expiation' and 'propitiation' is that 'expiation' signifies the cancellation of sin whereas 'propitiation' denotes the turning away of the wrath of God."[57] In this passage, (v. 14) we have already seen the death of Christ explained for the destruction of the devil's power over the people of God. Also, (v. 15) this action "paid" the slavery ransom debt freeing the people from the fear of death.

Ellingworth writes, "It is curious that the author should choose so unusual a term . . . and then apparently fail to develop it."[58] With humility, then, I prefer "conciliation" here rather than "propitiation" (ESV) or "expiation" for contextual-theological reasons. It is true in this passage there is repeated allusion to divine payment on behalf of the people of God. Further, there is ample textual evidence for this in other places in Hebrews (see below). However, in this passage the Lord's ministry as high priest described as "merciful and faithful" along with the forever freedom enjoyed by His people (cf. 7:23–25 below) seems to highlight His persistent ministry rather than His once-for-all atoning death. Additionally, coming to the help and the aid[59] of His people makes "conciliation" seem a more appropriate understanding of His service before the Lord in this verse.[60]

*Summary conclusion.*

This passage clearly illustrates the Lord took on blood and flesh, being made in our likeness so that He could undo the devil's enslaving power and conciliate before God on our behalf as our high priest. His actions here are on behalf of His people, indeed, as their representative-priest.

---

57. Allen, *Hebrews*, 224.
58. Ellingworth, *Hebrews*, 189.
59. BAGD, 144.
60. The challenge to this understanding is in seeing how conciliation works with "the sins of the people." To address this, I would connect His on-going conciliation with His on-going intercession (e.g., Rom 8:34; see below on 7:23–25).

Part Two | Typology Trajectory

Main Text B. "One who intercedes," Heb 7:23–25.

A second critical part of a priest's work is intercession for the people. In this text, intercession is a key component of the work of the Lord Jesus as our high priest. A translation of this passage is in Figure 3.

> [23]On the one hand, the priests that have come were many in number because death prevented continuing. [24]On the other hand, because [Jesus] remains forever, He has the permanent priesthood. [25]Therefore, also, those who draw near through Him to God, He is able to save to the uttermost; He always lives to make intercession for them.

**Figure 3.**

*The Argument.*

The Lord's Melchizedekian priesthood (the broader context of this passage) is in contrast to the Aaronic one. In Heb 5:6; 7:17, 20, the author cites Ps 110:4: "You are a priest forever, after the order of Melchizedek" and applies it to the Lord Jesus. What the author picks up in our passage is the wonderful implication of Jesus permanent priesthood for those who draw near to God, namely, He is always interceding on our behalf.

*Key words.*

Using the particles "on the one hand," 7:23, and "on the other," 7:24, the author creates a contrast between the priests of the old covenant and the high priest of the new (cf. 7:26).[61] Implicit in that contrast are the limitations of the former priests simply due to being human and fallen (e.g., 7:11, 27–28). The former priests that had come were hindered[62] in continuing in their office by their

---

61. See for example, Ellingworth, *Hebrews*, 390; Guthrie, *Hebrews*, 166.
62. *BAGD*, 461. Only occurrence in Hebrews.

death. The problem wasn't in the office but in the frailty of the office-holder. Death prevented the priests from continuing on in the ministry though the priesthood continued on. For our context, this is highly problematic because the holiness of God and the needs of God's people continue on—a vacant priesthood meant no advocacy for the people.

Unlike the former priests, the Lord remains forever, so He holds the priesthood permanently. Hebrews argues for a change in priesthood from Aaronic to Melchizedekian in Christ (cf. 8:6–7). With the eternal Christ as the high priest He is able to save to the uttermost, that is completely and fully.[63] This kind of high priest is precisely what the people of God need: not one who is frail unto death or bent unto sin but one who is eternal holding the priesthood forever. As above in chapter 2, the Lord's help came to Abraham's offspring (2:16); here they are called "those who draw near."[64] To them Christ died and for them He lives and, here, that "always living" means persistent intercession[65] on their behalf.

*Summary conclusion.*

The language of contrasts found in this passage supports the repeated usage of Ps 110:4 to describe the distinct priesthood of the Lord's, that is, eternal and unchanging. In our text, the author belabors Christ's eternal priesthood in making contrast with the forerunners (types). Further, the singular implication of Christ's forever appointment as high priest is His unending praying for His people. A priest is to advocate for the people before God; hardly a better proof of this as the Lord's role can be found.

---

63. *BAGD*, 608. Raymond Brown writes, "The phrase is doubtless a further reference to the far-reaching effects and unlimited adequacy of Christ's saving work." Brown, *Message of Hebrews*, 135.

64. Ellingworth notes this word is used in *Hebrews* of worship.

65. Notably this is the word used in Rom 8:27 (the Spirit's intercession) as well as 8:34 (the Lord's intercession).

Main text C. "One sacrifice to guarantee our standing," Heb 9:11–14.

While it is implicit with Melchizedek and explicit with Aaron and his sons, atoning and fellowship sacrifice were part of the normal role of the priest. The priest's role in preparing and offering sacrifice was necessary for the proper covenant relationship between God and man. What those sacrifices foreshadowed was a final, atoning sacrifice. In Heb 2:14, we already saw the intention of the Lord behind taking human blood and flesh was so that by His death He could overturn the power of the devil. This passage makes that process clear. A translation of our text is in Figure 4.

> [11]Christ, when He appeared a high priest of the good things that had come, through the greater and more complete tent (not one made by hands or that is of this earthly creation [12]neither through the blood of goats and calves but through His own blood), He entered, once for all, having attained the holy, eternal redemption. [13]For, if the blood of goats and bulls and ashes of a heifer being sprinkled on those who had been defiled is sanctifying the flesh for purification, [14]how much more the blood of Christ, that, through the eternal Spirit offered Himself without blemish to God, will purify our conscience from dead works to serve the God who is living.

**Figure 4.**

## *The Argument.*

To this point in chapter 9, the author summarizes the activities of the old covenant priests and the high priests (cf. 8:13). At the same time, he highlights the priests could only go so far and the high priest (only on an annual basis) went into the Holy of Holies. Though mandated by the covenant regulations, the offerings of the priest and high priest acted for the souls of the worshippers in a limited way. Our text explains the Lord appeared as a different kind of priest having entered through a different kind of tent with

## Jesus the Messiah: Archetype Prophet, Priest, and King

a different kind of offering and, if the former priests through the earthly tent (i.e., tabernacle) with earthly offerings sanctified the worshipper, how much more will the offering of Christ save to the uttermost?

### Key words.

"Christ" falls as the first word in the text. This is significant as the author's argument to this point is about priests, more specifically high priests. For the author to put "Christ" as the first word is somewhat shocking.[66] Christ "when He appeared"[67] is described as "of the good things that had come." Swiftly moving, the author doesn't define this phrase but intends it to summarize what he will unpack further, namely, aspects of the different tent, offering and effects.[68]

He first discusses the tent and Christ's relation to it. Christ as high priest is described as having come "through" ("by means of") the "greater and more complete" tent. "Greater" and "more complete" tent is described further as one neither "made with hands" nor of earthly creation. This tent was not made by man of earthly things (cf. Mark 14:58; Acts 7:48).[69] The "tent" draws the reader in two directions. First, back to 9:2-5, descriptions of the tabernacle established for Mosaic covenantal worship. But, subsequent to our text, the author combines these concepts saying the "tent" the Lord has entered is heaven itself (9:24) to offer Himself once for all (9:24, 25).[70] In our text, he is slow walking a contrast between the tents of 9:2ff and 9:23ff by explaining what the Lord entered was not the same as what the high priest entered.

---

66. "Nowhere else in Hebrews does (Christōs) alone stand at the beginning of a sentence much less a major division" Ellingworth, *Hebrews*, 448.

67. Louw and Nida, *Greek-English Lexicon*, 192–93.

68. Ellingworth suggests the author intends possession of greater value than the promised land; *Hebrews*, 450.

69. Wilson, *Hebrews*, 116.

70. Bruce, *Hebrews*, 212.

Next, the author moves to contrast the nature of the sacrifices in these two tents. In verse 12, the offerings of the one tent involved the blood of goats and calves (cf. Lev 16:3) but it was not by those means did the Lord enter into the greater and more complete tent. Rather, "by His own blood He entered" that is "by virtue of His own blood."[71] The author stresses the Lord went in with His own blood to give.[72] Nor did He enter repeatedly as the former priests but once.[73]

The effect of His entering by His own blood into the Holy of Holies[74] was the "attaining" of "eternal redemption." "Attaining" in the middle voice seems to be similar to "grasping to himself" or "taking to himself" as one would choose an object. "Obtained" (e.g., NASB, HCSB, NIV) is better than "securing" (ESV). What the Lord obtained ("eternal redemption"[75]) by His own blood resembles His character (cf. Hebrews 5:9, 9:15; see esp. 1 John 5:20). The same could not be said of the blood offerings made by the high priests of old.

Lastly, he explains the differences of effects of these sacrifices. In verses 13–14, using contrast, the author shows the more exalted effectiveness of Christ's one sacrifice. He already explained (9:9–10) the former sacrifices could not "perfect" the conscience but only deal with regulations for the body. Here (9:13) he extends this further by saying the ones who have been ceremonially defiled[76]

---

71. Bruce, *Hebrews*, 213. With the contrast of the type of blood, it is possible this is an attributive genitive, instead.

72. "With" His own blood shouldn't be understood that He carried, as the priests before Him, some other blood. He came with Himself as the sacrifice; the blood He carried, He carried in His veins. See, for example, Rom 5:9.

73. Romans 6:10, "For the death he died he died to sin, once for all, but the life he lives he lives to God."

74. NA$^{27}$ capitalizes "Holy of Holies" (*hagia hagiōn*) in 9:3 but neither uses the same form here (*ta hagia*) nor puts it in capital letters. However, the proximity to 9:3 could mean the author intends this also to mean the holy of holies.

75. "To release or set free, with the implied analogy to the process of freeing a slave." Louw and Nida, *Greek-English Lexicon*, 487.

76. BAGD, 438. "The language is used of defilement both under the old and new dispensations," Ellingworth, *Hebrews*, 455.

## Jesus the Messiah: Archetype Prophet, Priest, and King

had the blood of goats and bulls and the ashes of heifers sprinkled on them and their flesh (cf. "body" 9:10) and are purified.

This is set in contrast by layering the exalted nature of Christ's cleansing blood. It begins with the evocative "how much more" anchoring the author's intent to say greater things about the Lord. It is the blood Christ (cf. 1 Cor 10:16) offered Himself through[77] the eternal Spirit[78] a sacrifice without blemish that will purify[79] our consciences (cf. 9:9). Ellingworth answers why the agency of the Spirit is combined with the Lord offering His own blood, "it was the power of the eternal Spirit which enabled Christ to be at the same time both high priest and offering."[80] Purification of the flesh for appearance before the presence of the Lord at the tabernacle is contrasted with the deeper purification of the conscience from dead works by Christ's blood. God's people are purified to serve (that is, "worship" cf. e.g., 9:9, 10:2) the God who is living.

*Summary conclusion.*

This is only one text in Hebrews explaining the Lord Jesus offered Himself as final and single sacrifice for the sins of His people, "But as it is, he has appeared once for all at the end of the ages to put away sin by the sacrifice of himself. And just as it is appointed for man to die once, and after that comes judgment, so Christ, having been offered once to bear the sins of many, will appear a second time, not to deal with sin but to save those who are eagerly waiting for him" (9:26-28).

---

77. "The genitive substantive indicates the personal agent by whom the action in view is accomplished." Wallace, *Basics of New Testament Syntax*, 61.

78. The Holy Spirit. See Ellingworth, *Hebrews*, 457.

79. *BAGD*, 387, used figuratively for "moral and religious cleansing." For example, in Lev 12:7-8 (LXX), this verb is used along with atonement for sins; cf. Lev 16:30.

80. Ellingworth, *Hebrews*, 457.

## Conclusion.

The Westminster Shorter Catechism, Q. 25 asks, "How does Christ execute the office of a priest?" The answer, "Christ executes the office of a priest in His once offering up of Himself a sacrifice to satisfy divine justice and reconcile us to God and in making continual intercession for us."[81]

The Lord Jesus as our great high priest is proved in three important ways. As our priest, He must be like us, that is, having taken on human flesh. We see this truth proved in 2:14–18. Secondly, as the priests of old, He would have to engage in the ministry of intercession. That He has this ministry eternally is proved in 7:23–25. Lastly, priests ministered before the Lord with blood. In ways far above all other priests, in ministry far greater than theirs, the Lord Jesus, by His blood has become our sacrifice.

## SECTION 3: JESUS AS THE REIGNING KING: LUKE 1:32–33[82]

### Introduction

The confession, "Jesus is Lord," is common in the New Testament (e.g., Acts 10:36; Rom 10:9; Phil 2:11). In its simplest definition, for Jesus to be "Lord" means upon Him was given the right and authority to rule the church as her Head (Col 1:18).[83] He received this role upon His baptism (Matt 3:16–17), He proved His worthiness for this role by His overcoming the temptation to abuse it

---

81. Beeke and Ferguson, *Reformed Confessions Harmonized*, 71.

82. "What then is the rock bottom of the faith of the primitive Church? It is expressed in two words, *Jesous Kurios*, 'Jesus Is Lord.' As we dig down deeper and deeper into the strata of the tradition, we come finally to that simple affirmation." Visser t' Hooft, *Kingship of Christ*, 67, cited in Sherman, *King, Priest, and Prophet*, 117.

83. Beale and Carson, *Commentary on the New Testament Use of the Old Testament*, 220. Since my thesis regards the Archetype-Ectype framework, I will not consider Jesus' lordship over all of creation.

## Jesus the Messiah: Archetype Prophet, Priest, and King

(Matt 4:11),[84] and by His perfect law-abiding (Heb 4:15, cf. Matt 11:27, 28:18) and sealed it with His resurrection (e.g., Col 2:15).

Jesus did not refuse the title when it was applied to Him (e.g., Matt 3:3, 7:21–22; Mark 2:28; John 1:49, 20:28). It is certainly the case, after His ascension, the apostles and NT authors recognized Him as Lord and King. The text we will consider is Luke 1:31–33. A translation of our passage is in Figure 5.

| Verse | Line | |
|---|---|---|
| 31 | 1 | And behold |
| | 2 | You will conceive |
| | 3 | in the womb |
| | 4 | (And) you will birth |
| | 5 | A son |
| | 6 | (And) you will call |
| | 7 | His name, Jesus. |
| 32 | 8 | (a) He will be great, and |
| | 9 | (b) He will be called, "Son of the Most High," and |
| | 10 | (c) The Lord God will give to Him |
| | 11 | The throne of His father, David, and |
| 33 | 12 | (d) He will reign |
| | 13 | Over the house of Jacob |
| | 14 | Forever, and |
| | 15 | (e) Of His kingdom, there will be no end |

**Figure 5.**

### Commentary.

Prior to our text, in this part of the larger narrative (1:26–38), the angel Gabriel has approached Mary greeting her in a startling way, "Greetings, O favored one, the Lord is with you!" While her response indicated she was "greatly troubled,"[85] the angel reassured

---

84. See also Sherman, *King, Priest and Prophet*, 110–11.
85. Louw and Nida, *Greek-English Lexicon*, 314.

## Part Two | Typology Trajectory

her of his intentions with another salutation forming an *inclusio* with the first, " . . . you have found favor with God."[86] The angel's message has three parts. The first (1:26–30) regards the fact that Mary will conceive and give birth to a son. The second (1:31–33) answers the question, "Who will He be?" And the third (1:34–38) will address Mary's curiosity on how she will conceive as an unmarried woman.

*Lines 1–7 (v. 31). "And behold, you will conceive in the womb, you will birth a son; you will call His name, Jesus."*

In rapid fire, through three future verbs, Luke narrates three facts. Mary, "you will conceive,"[87] "you will birth a son,"[88] and "you will call His name, Jesus." At this point, it is clear, the fulfillment of Isaiah's prophecy is upon her, "Therefore the Lord himself will give you a sign. Behold, the virgin shall conceive and bear a son, and shall call his name 'Immanuel'" (Isa 7:14). Indeed, on the angel's approach and message, Green suggests we hear an "echo" of Isa 7:10–17.[89] Regarding the last fact, the boy's name, Luke does not dwell on the significance of His name (cf. Matthew 1:21) but rather rolls right into describing the significance of the Son Himself, namely, He will be King. What follows is a unified five-fold description of Jesus as King (held together with the coordinate conjunction "and").

*Line 8 (v.32). "He will be great."*

In these origin narratives, Luke has already described John the Baptist as "great before the Lord" (1:15). For John to be "great before the Lord" meant "great in the eyes of the Lord"[90] since his

---

86. Green, *Luke*, 86.
87. *BAGD*, 776.
88. *BAGD*, 816.
89. Green, *Luke*, 85.
90. Marshall, *Luke*, 57.

## Jesus the Messiah: Archetype Prophet, Priest, and King

special ordination (1:15, 41), mission, and his dedication were above all men (Luke 7:28; cf. Matthew 11:11). Luke doesn't expand on describing Jesus as "great" though BAGD lists its possible usage as figuratively describing "rank or dignity."[91]

Having this descriptor tied to the other four, more detailed (and exalted) descriptions supports the idea that Luke is conveying greatness of rank or dignity. It is also possible "great" without further descriptions may be used to modify God alone, or as "absolute" greatness.[92]

### Line 9 (v. 32). "And, He will be called, 'Son of the Most High.'"

Gabriel has already instructed both Joseph (Matt 1:21) and Mary, the Child's name would be "Jesus." In Matthew (unlike here), the angel further connects His birth to the fulfillment of the Isaianic prophecy (7:14). Perhaps here, as with Luke's use of "great," we are to understand a measure of His greatness. That as "Jesus," to us, He is truly the "Son of the Most High." Geldenhuys notes the parallels between John's "great before the Lord" and Jesus' "great and will be called the Son of the Most High." In this way, he sees Luke giving more definition to the Lord's greatness.[93]

In verse 32, "Son of the Most High" is in the emphatic as it is placed before the verb. This description of God is found almost exclusively in Luke-Acts.[94] The use of "Most High" in the Old Testament refers to God's supreme authority. Genesis 14:19, "And [Melchizedek] blessed [Abram] and said, "Blessed be Abram by God Most High, Possessor of heaven and earth." In Num 24:16

---

91. *BAGD*, 498.

92. Bock, *Luke*, 113. Though Bock produces examples where *megas* is used alone and not used of God (e.g., Exod 11:3; Esth 10:3). Marshall seems to differ slightly, "The title is more than a name; it indicates the true being of the person so called. The title is equivalent to the more common 'Son of God.'" Marshall, *Luke*, 66.

93. Geldenhuys, *Gospel of Luke*, 167.

94. Luke 1:32, 35, 76; 6:35; 8:28; Acts 7:48; 16:17. In Mark 5:7, it is on the lips of a legion of demons resisting the Lord Jesus and, in Heb 7:1, it is the one whom Melchizedek served.

Part Two | Typology Trajectory

(as Gen 14:19), what the LXX translates is "most high or highest."[95] Taken together with 1:35, "Son of the Most High" is synonymous with "Son of God," a circumlocution for God.[96]

*Lines 10–11 (v. 32). "And, the Lord God will give to Him, the throne of His father, David."*

To this point in the narrative, Gabriel relates to Mary the greatness of her Son, that is, He is the Son of the most high, God Himself. As if to localize the wonder of this fact, he further explains, as in the early days of the nation, the Son will be King over the people of the line of David: "the throne of His father, David" clearly implies His kingship (cf. Mark 1:15).

Luke doesn't expand on the contours of this kingdom, however, a brief consideration of the covenant promise in 2 Sam 7:11–16 will bear out these details. In 2 Sam 7:11–16, the Lord covenants with David to perpetually seat his kin on his throne to rule Israel through the ages. Consider the comparison below in Figure 6.

| Luke | | 2 Samuel 11 | |
|---|---|---|---|
| 1:32 | "He will be great" | 11:9 | "I will make for you a great name" |
| 1:32 | "The Lord God will give to him the throne of His father, David" | 11:12 | "I will raise up your offspring after you" |
| | | | "I will establish his kingdom" |
| | | 11:13 | "I will establish the throne of his kingdom forever" |
| | "[He] will be called the Son of the Most High" | 11:14 | "I will be to him a father and he shall be to me a son" |
| 1:33 | "He will reign over the house of Jacob forever" | 11:16 | "And your kingdom shall be made sure forever before me" |
| | "And of His kingdom, there will be no end" | | "Your throne shall be established forever." |

**Figure 6**

95. Brown et al., *Hebrew and English Lexicon*, 751.
96. Stein, *Luke*, 83–84.

*Jesus the Messiah: Archetype Prophet, Priest, and King*

References to this covenantal promise are also found in Ps 89 and 110 (also 132:10-11). In Ps 89:3-4 we read, "I have made a covenant with My chosen one; I have sworn to David My servant: I will establish your offspring forever, and build your throne for all generations." And in verses 36-37, "Once for all I have sworn by My holiness; I will not lie to David. His offspring shall endure forever, his throne as long as the sun before Me. Like the moon, it shall be established forever, a faithful witness in the skies."

Psalm 110:1-2 confirms the covenant promise, "'The LORD said to my Lord: sit at My right hand, until I make Your enemies Your footstool.' The Lord sends forth from Zion Your mighty scepter. Rule in the midst of your enemies."[97] Isaiah 9:6-7 is also supporting text for Luke's statements here:

> For to us a Child is born; to us a Son is given; and the government shall be upon His shoulder; and His name shall be called, Wonderful Counselor, Mighty God, Everlasting Father, Prince of Peace. Of the increase of His government and of peace there will be no end, on the throne of David and over his kingdom, to establish it and to uphold it with justice and with righteousness from this time forth and forevermore. The zeal of the Lord of hosts will do this.

In Gabriel's words to Mary, we have fulfillment of the Davidic covenantal promise in lines 10-11 (1:32b).[98]

*Lines 12-15 (v. 33).* "*And, He will reign over the house of Jacob forever and of His kingdom, there will be no end.*"

Not only are these the fourth and fifth descriptive phrases Luke uses to describe the Lord's kingship, it signifies the result of God giving the Son His throne, namely, He will rule over His people

---

97. This is cited in oblique reference to the Lord Jesus in Matt 22:44 (cf. Mark 12:36, Luke 20:42-43). In Acts 2:34-35 and Heb 1:13 the link is unquestionable.

98. Bock, *Luke*, 114.

forever.⁹⁹ His kingdom will be over the "house of Jacob," that is a circumlocution for those who fall under the covenant the Lord made with Jacob (through Isaac, through Abraham). In other words, only the spiritual descendants of Abraham will reside in the kingdom (cf. Gal. 3:7–9).

Different than the covenantal promise of a line of succession for David's faithful sons, Luke isn't teaching the Davidic kingdom will continue, but that a Davidic-type king will come and, as He is eternal, so also will be His kingship. As Bock says, "Nothing will overcome Jesus or bring His reign to a halt."¹⁰⁰

## Conclusion.

Gabriel's announcement to Mary powerfully wove OT covenantal threads together. Her Son will be "great," as predicted. He will be God in the flesh. He comes thusly to inherit what was prophesied as His own: David's kingdom. He will not simply rule over spiritual Israel as the next king, but His kingdom is eternal as He is eternal.

---

99. Green, *Luke*, 88. See also Daniel 7:14 for another possible supporting text.

100. Bock, *Luke*, 117; Marshall, *Luke*, 68; Calvin and Pringle, *Matthew, Mark and Luke*, 2:2:39.

# CHAPTER FOUR

## The Promise and Provision of "Greater Works"

> "Truly, truly, I say to you, whoever believes in Me will also do the works that I do; and greater works than these will he do, because I am going to the Father. Whatever you ask in My name, this I will do, that the Father may be glorified in the Son. If you ask Me anything in My name, I will do it."
>
> JOHN 14:12–14

THE HEART OF THIS project is the deployment of local church members in ministry according to the biblical framework of the prophet, priest, and king (PPK). In other words, to assist church members gifted by the Holy Spirit in building on the finished work of Christ as "ectypes" of Christ; to serve the Lord in the same manner as Christ did His work: in prophetic, priestly, and kingly efforts.

This involves the "promise" of greater works, the "provision" for greater works, and the "practice" of greater works. The biblical logic for this is as follows:

Part Two | Typology Trajectory

1. The Promise. In John 14:12–14, the Lord Jesus promises the church will continue His works and do greater works still.
2. The Provision. In Eph 4:7–12, the apostle Paul teaches that the ascended Lord Jesus gives some believers certain foundational spiritual gifts in order to train the church for the work of ministry.[1]
3. The Practice. Trained by those foundationally gifted (as in above), the well-known gift list passages in Rom 12, 1 Cor 12 and 1 Pet 4 outline the synergistic work of the Spirit working through the church in spiritual gifts classified according to the PPK.

In this chapter, we will consider the promise of greater works and the provision for the church to do the greater works. In the next chapter, we will consider the practice of those greater works.

## SECTION 1: THE PROMISE OF GREATER WORKS: JOHN 14:12–14

In the "Upper Room Discourse," the Lord Jesus taught numerous astounding truths to His disciples. Among them is the idea that they, and those with a faith like theirs, will do the works of the Lord and "greater works" even than those.

The essential challenge in properly understanding this statement is to see these works as the application of or building upon Christ's finished work and not works due to the incomplete nature of Christ's saving work.[2] Indeed, in summary form on the cross, the Lord Himself stated His works were finished (John 19:30). What remains is the application of the redemption earned by the Lord's active and passive obedience. That application would be

---

1. We will also consider a brief look at the person and work of the Holy Spirit—the true Provision.
2. Andreas Köstenberger describes this as "not in duplicating Jesus' mission or task, but in bearing witness to it as Jesus' representatives." Köstenberger, "Greater Works of the Believer," 39; McGraw, "Theology of Corporate Prayer," 170.

## The Promise and Provision of "Greater Works"

done through the agency of the Holy Spirit and the action of the local church. The Lord speaks this by way of promise to the disciples in John 14:12–14.

### Introduction

"Lord, where are You going?" The apostle Peter had a number of questions for the Lord in the Upper Room. Jesus' answer to this one was not comforting, "Where I am going you cannot follow Me now but you will follow afterward" (John 13:36). Andreas Köstenberger summarizes the complex nature of Jesus' actions and His words in the Upper Room in writing, "The underlying logic of the Farewell Discourse is that, counterintuitively, not only would the disciples not be seriously disadvantaged by Jesus' imminent departure, but it would actually be better for them if Jesus went away."[3]

In John's gospel, the Upper Room Discourse (John 13–17) contains Jesus' last words and action with His disciples. Here we find Him serving them (e.g., 13:1–12), teaching them (e.g., 14:1, 15; 15:4, 12), warning them (e.g., 15:18–21), encouraging them (e.g., 14:15–19, 27), and praying for them (17:1–26). Through these scenes, He reveals more of Himself (e.g., 14:10), His Father (e.g., 14:7–8), and His glory (e.g., 17:1). In one poignant scene, after the departure of Judas Iscariot, He declares His glorification is at hand.

In a veiled way, He speaks of His ascension and states, "Little children, yet a little while I am with you. You will seek Me and just as I said to the Jews, so now I also say to you, 'Where I am going, you cannot come'" (John 13:33).[4] This provokes questions from Peter, Thomas, and Philip, respectively. Through these, He begins a discourse following this logic:

1. You will be staying for now
2. Do not be troubled
3. You have work to do

---

3. Kostenberger, *Signs of the Messiah*, 148.
4. Carson, *The Gospel According to John*, 483.

## Part Two | Typology Trajectory

"You will be staying for now." Underneath this discourse is the constant theme of the unfinished work of the disciples. The Upper Room Discourse makes a clear case for the on-going presence and work of His people in the world. Whether it is how they must live together (e.g., 13:34, 15:12), how they must live with Him (e.g., 15:1–4) or how they can expect to be treated by the world (e.g., 15:18–21), they will not be following Him "now" but rather staying.

"Do not be troubled . . .. You have work to do." As expected, the talk of His departure and their remaining troubles them (e.g., 14:1, 27; 16:22). Peter wants to know why he cannot follow (13:37). Thomas despairs of not knowing the way to be with Jesus again (14:5). And Philip, eager to "see" the Father, asks Jesus for the beatific vision (14:8). This sets up the last move in the logic above. While the disciples have understandable concerns about being absent from the Lord, He responds with the exhortation that they have work to do that requires His absence.

John 14:12–14 may be translated according to Figure 1:

| Verse | Line | |
|---|---|---|
| 12 | 1 | Truly, truly I say to you all |
|  | 2 | The one believing in Me |
|  | 3 | The works |
|  | 4 | That I am doing |
|  | 5 | Also he will |
|  | 6 | Do |
|  | 7 | And greater than these |
|  | 8 | He will do |
|  | 9 | Because I, to the Father, am going |
| 13 | 10 | And what you all may ask in My name this |
|  | 11 | I will do |
|  | 12 | So that the Father may be glorified in the Son |
| 14 | 13 | If anything you all ask Me in My name |
|  | 14 | I myself will do |

**Figure 1.**

*The Promise and Provision of "Greater Works"*

# Commentary

*Line 1 (v. 12). "Truly, truly, I say to you all . . ."*

Using Semitic idiom extremely common in John's gospel, Jesus uses an oath formula to certify what He is saying is true.[5] "I tell you the truth" (NIV) is an accurate way to understand this opening as "truly" (lit. "amen"). It comes from the Hebrew root word that means "surely" or "certainly" (e.g., Deut 27:15–19). In this manner of address, the Lord also transitioned from speaking to individual disciples (e.g., Peter: 13:36, Thomas: 14:6, and Philip: 14:9) to addressing them as a group.

*Line 2. "The one believing in Me"*[6]

Rather than referring to one who once had faith, Jesus is speaking of a person standing in his faith. The context does not seem to restrict the referent to only the assembled disciples. In other words, anyone at any time who is believing in Jesus is about whom Jesus refers.[7]

Jesus has already used the verb "believe" in His discourse with the disciples. In response to the sorrow of the disciples over Jesus' impending departure, He tells them, "Let not your hearts be troubled. Believe in God; believe also in Me" (14:1). His response to Philip's request to see the Father was, "Believe in Me that I am in the Father and the Father is in Me or else believe on account of the works themselves" (14:11). Here, "believe" is best understood not as believe "about," that is, putting trust in a set of propositions rather to believe "in" or having "faith in the Divinity that lays special emphasis on trust in his power and his nearness to help in

---

5. This is found twenty-five times overall, seven in the Upper Room Discourse alone. Carson, *John*, 162.

6. I take this as a progressive or descriptive present. See Wallace, 222; Hendriksen, *Gospel According to John*, 277.

7. Carson, *John*, 495; Borchert, *John 12–21*, 115.

Part Two | Typology Trajectory

addition to being convinced that he exists and that his revelations or disclosures are true."[8]

## Lines 3-4. *"The works that I am doing"*

John gives no specific detail about the works, that is, exactly what is specified. John's use of the word "sign" in his gospel seems to preclude equating them with the "works" he means here.[9] In John, "signs" are normally miraculous works attesting primarily to the Jews of the coming of their Messiah. The debates around "cessationism" notwithstanding, following John's terminology here can simplify our understanding of how the post-resurrection church can be said to do Jesus' works rather than His signs.

Therefore works may be defined simply as "that which is done, with possible focus on the energy or effort involved—'act, deed.'"[10] This general definition is also seen in *The Theological Dictionary of the New Testament*:

> The words may be used of agriculture and agricultural economy, but also of the pursuit of various trades, of all kinds of occupations, of commercial undertakings, of trade, shipping and fishing (Rev. 18:17), of the chase, and of art, sculpture and poetry. They may also be applied to working in various materials (metal, wood, stone, clay), or the fashioning or erection of various objects such as vessels or buildings, or all kinds of technical or cultural works, including the winning of natural products, For these varied possibilities there are several examples in the Gk. Bible. The terms also denote work in the social or ethical sense either as a burden laid on man or as a necessary means of life and support. They are applied no

---

8. *BAGD*, 661.

9. John uses this word seventeen times in his gospel, though not at all in the Upper Room Discourse. *BAGD* defines *semeion*, "sign," as either a distinguishing mark by which something is known or as a miracle, 747–748. See also Köstenberger, "Greater Works of the Believer," 37–39. Contra McGraw, "Theology of Corporate Prayer," 172.

10. Louw and Nida, *Greek-English Lexicon*, 307. Hereafter *LN*.

## The Promise and Provision of "Greater Works"

less to the domestic tasks of woman than to the public work of men.[11]

Grant Osborne explains "works" here as "all the 'works' of Jesus: his deeds of servanthood and love, his proclamation of divine truths, his life of piety and prayer, and his power to change the lives of those around him."[12] In John's gospel, he uses "work" (or "works" or "working") twenty-six times. With the large range of specific meaning, what "work" means in an occurrence must be defined by its context. It is activity but the nature of the activity is context-specific.

In the Upper Room Discourse, the word "work" is used five (5) times: John 14:10, 11, 12; 15:24 and 17:4. John 15:24, for example, is a warning to the disciples who will do ministry in the world, "If I had not done among them the works that no one else did, they would not be guilty of sin, but now they have seen and hated both Me and My Father." The nature of the works here is unspecified. We can deduce from the world's response of hatred, the works Christ did exposed the sinfulness and lostness of the world (1 John 2:15-17, cf. Rom 12:2).

John 17:4 is very different. In Jesus high priestly prayer, He prayed, "I glorified You on earth, having accomplished the work that You gave Me to do." These are those kingdom tasks the Father had given Him to do (4:34, cf. 5:36). Carson doesn't believe these works can be restricted to deeds of humility, acts of love or the preaching of the gospel.[13] Neither does it follow these "works" (literally, "things") only include Jesus' active perfect obedience to the Law of God that would be the basis upon which the elect are saved from their sins (e.g., 17:4).[14] In the other occurrences of "work" in John, context does give some indication about their character: e.g. evil works: 7:7, 8:41 or miraculous works: 5:1-8. In the end, Gerald

---

11. Georg Bertram, "work" word group in Kittel, Bromiley, and Friedrich, *Theological Dictionary of the New Testament*, 635.
12. Osborne, *Luke*, 339-340; italics mine.
13. Carson, *John*, 495.
14. He would not tell the disciples they would continue that work.

Borchert translates this verse as, "I tell you the truth, anyone who has faith in me *will do what I have been doing.*"[15]

## Lines 5-8. "Also he will do and greater than these he will do"

From the moment Jesus spoke these words, He instructed the disciples work remained to be done and this work would resemble what they had witnessed in Him. Who is "he" who would do this work? The one who believes. Just as Jesus spoke in general terms about those who were believing in Him not restricting it to the apostles alone, neither does He do so here. The one who believes will "also" do the works Jesus was doing.

Jesus tells us the works He did will be the "source code," so to speak, for the works and greater works of those who believe in Him. Based on John's usage it does not appear Jesus has in mind completely new or different works.[16] (Indeed our context will not allow that conclusion.) Jesus' works were those the Father gave to Him (John 4:34). If they are the source code for the works of all who believe in Him, what might they entail for us?

1. Works that bear witness Christ is the Messiah doing the work of God.[17] John 5:36:

   "But the testimony that I have is greater than that of John. For the works that the Father has given me to accomplish, the very works that I am doing, bear witness about me that the Father has sent me."

2. Works that facilitate gospel proclamation and faith.[18] John 6:28-29:

---

15. Borchert, *John 12-21*, 115, emphasis added.
16. Ramsey agrees, "The reference to 'believing' and to 'the works I am doing' signal that the subject matter has not changed." Ramsey, *Gospel of John*, 779.
17. Ramsey, *John*, 329.
18. Carson, *John*, 285; Milne, *Message of John*, 110.

## The Promise and Provision of "Greater Works"

> Then they said to him, "What must we do, to be doing the works of God?" Jesus answered them, "This is the work of God, that you believe in him whom he has sent."

3. Works that display the compassion and mercy of God. John 9:3–5:

> Jesus answered, "It was not that this man sinned, or his parents, but that the works of God might be displayed in him. We must work the works of him who sent me while it is day; night is coming, when no one can work. As long as I am in the world, I am the light of the world."

4. Works that reveal the good character and intention of the Father.[19] John 10:32:

> Jesus answered them, "I have shown you many good works from the Father; for which of them are you going to stone me?"

In a word, prophetic works, priestly works, and kingly works. Still, for the church to do these works doesn't seem "greater." Indeed Jesus told them, "And greater than these he will do." Carson doesn't believe it simply means "more" since there are other words in the Greek to express such a concept.[20] However, Ramsey states "more" might very well be Jesus' meaning due to the limited scope of Jesus' ministry, "We have known all along that he had a limited time to complete his works."[21] What makes the disciples doing these "greater" than Jesus doing them is connected to Jesus' reason for charging them in the first place, "because, to the Father, I am going."

---

19. Ramsey, *John*, 601; Bruce, *Gospel and Epistles of John*, 233.
20. Carson, *John*, 495. Nor does he think it means "more spectacular" or "supernatural."
21. Ramsey, *John*, 780.

Part Two | Typology Trajectory

*Line 9. "Because, to the Father, I am going."*

In this way, Jesus speaks both of His ascension and His destination.[22] In John's usage of the phrase, it is often challenging to know exactly which is specified though it might be a distinction without a meaningful difference. The germane point is that He will no longer be physically with the disciples as He would return to the Father.

This phrase is key in this passage for two reasons. First, it is important because we find out why He tells the disciples they will do the work that He was doing and greater works still: He is physically leaving them. His physical departure signals the conclusion of a necessary phase of His work and the beginning of another, that is, the application of His work to the elect throughout time and history until His second return, "You will be staying and there is work to do."

Second, the works and greater works will be possible since He will be shortly glorified, that is, ascended, seated at God's right hand and, with the Father, sending the Holy Spirit to reside and work through all who put their faith in Christ.[23] "Nevertheless, I tell you the truth: it is to your advantage that I go away, for if I do not go away, the Helper will not come to you, But if I go, I will send him to you" (John 16:7).

"Greater," then, is eschatological. His resurrection and ascension (and especially Pentecost) will inaugurate an era that includes far more expansive kingdom growth and development than what He accomplished in His first advent.[24] In a word, "greater." A helpful and non-context driven definition of "greater" is: an intensification in impact, in number, in scope or in size.[25]

---

22. John 13:1, 14:6, 14:12, 14:28, 16:10, 16:17, 16:28, 20:17. Köstenberger calls this a "euphemism for his crucifixion and resurrection." "Greater Works of the Believer," 14:1–12, 40.

23. John 14:16, 18, 26; 15:26.

24. R. V. G. Tasker says the works are "not greater in kind than those of Jesus, but greater in the sphere of influence." Tasker, *John*, 17; Köstenberger, "Greater Works of the Believer," 40; Ramsey, *John*, 780; Carson, *John*, 496.

25. "A measure of intensity," *BAGD*, 497; "the upper range of a scale of

## The Promise and Provision of "Greater Works"

The eschaton, the time between the first and second comings of Christ, will be a time of greater kingdom work, that is, in impact, in depth, in size, and in scope. The continuity we have already seen in Jesus' words (i.e., "the works that I am doing, also he will do") indicate "greater" works could simply be "what Jesus has done so far and what he will do (through [the disciples]) by "going to the Father."[26] George R. Beasley-Murray captures this: "The disciples go forth to their mission and seek the Lord's aid therein and in response to their prayers *he* will do through them 'greater things' than in the days of his flesh, 'that the Father may be glorified in the Son"—in the powerful mission that *he* continues."[27] Grundmann says, "This going to the Father gives Him the possibility of greater efficacy exercised through the disciples."[28] Again, "greater works" are kingdom works that either are the same as Jesus had done or are appropriate applications of what Jesus had done such that the impact is more intensified (in scope or reach) than even those same types of works done by Jesus Himself.

*Lines 10–12 (v.13). "And what you all may ask in My name, this I will do so that the Father may be glorified in the Son."*

This phrase does not introduce a different topic (i.e., prayer) but emphasizes to the disciples what He has just told them they will do will be done in cooperation with the risen and seated Lord Himself. The connection is found as displayed in Figure 1 above: these lines from verse 13 restate what Jesus has already stated, that is, "what you all may ask" is restating the works and greater works of the disciples.

Prayer, ". . .in My name," is key connective tissue here. "My works" plus "greater works" plus "My name" is a clear message of the centrality of the will and work of Jesus even as He leaves the

---

extent," *LN*, 684.

26. Ramsey, *John*, 780.

27. Beasley-Murray, *John*, 380. Emphasis in original.

28. Walter Grundmann, "mega" ("greater") word group in *Theological Dictionary of the New Testament*, 537.

## Part Two | Typology Trajectory

disciples. John uses this phrase exclusively in the Upper Room Discourse.[29] In verse 13 (its first usage) it can be understood as a general exhortation and encouragement. "In My name" means according to all that His name stands for.[30] Ramsey adds, "'Ask as if I were asking' or 'Ask what I would ask.'"[31]

"This I will do." "This" here isn't a blanket statement (cf. 15:7) but refers back to "what you all may ask in My name." Importantly, it must also refer to the works that "I am doing" (12:12a) and the "greater works" they will do (12:12b).[32] These all hang together. We cannot properly think through these future works without recognizing they are in continuity with the works Jesus had been doing in His role as our Mediator, works done according to the offices of prophet, priest, and king.

What the Lord had been doing in His humiliation He will continue to do in His exaltation, that is, works according to the offices of prophet, priest, and king.[33] The discontinuity is now these works will be done prayerfully in Jesus' name by His disciples. Therefore, when Jesus says, "This I will do," He is affirming part of His mediatorial work in the offices will have passed to His Spirit-endowed people.

"So that the Father may be glorified in the Son." To glorify is to "speak of something as being unusually fine and deserving honor."[34] This commitment to esteem the Father above all, to keep His glory uppermost is a regular feature of the Lord's words and

---

29. John 14:13, 14, 26; 15:16; 16:23, 24, 26.

30. Carson, *John*, 497. Hendricksen adds such prayers are "in the interest of God's kingdom. . . .a prayer in Christ's name is a prayer that is in harmony with whatever Christ has revealed concerning himself," Hendricksen, *John*, 274.

31. Ramsey, *John*, 782.

32. Ramsey, *John*, 781.

33. *Westminster Shorter Catechism*, Question 23 says, "What offices does Christ execute as our Redeemer?" "Christ, as our Redeemer, executes the offices of a prophet, of a priest and of a king, *both* in His estate of humiliation *and exaltation*." Beeke and Ferguson, eds., *Reformed Confessions Harmonized*, 69; emphasis added; see also proof texts included.

34. *LN*, 429.

## The Promise and Provision of "Greater Works"

work. He implied this already several times in John's Gospel: 5:44; 7:18; 8:50, 54. In other places, He is explicit about the Father's glory:

1. John 12:28, in Jesus' time of trouble over the mission: "Father, glorify Your name."
2. John 15:8, to the disciples: "By this my Father is glorified, that you bear much fruit and so prove to be my disciples."
3. John 17:1–5, to the Father: "Father, the hour has come; glorify your Son that the Son may glorify you, since you have given him authority over all flesh, to give eternal life to all whom you have given him . . .. I glorified you on earth, having accomplished the work that you gave me to do. And now, Father, glorify me in your own presence with the glory that I had with you before the world existed."

In our verse, when the disciples do the works and greater works of the Lord prayerfully in His name, Jesus has pledged to empower those works ("do" them by virtue of His Spirit, on which see below) so that the Father is glorified. That is, so those impacted by them would sing songs of praise of and to the Father in heaven. The logic of this verse is wonderful: with the glory of the Father uppermost for the Son, prayer requests in the Son's name to do the works of God are certain to be accomplished!

*Lines 13–14 (v.14). "If anything you all ask Me, in My name, I myself will do."*

The repetition of pronouns in the verse is challenging: "Me," "My" and "I myself."[35] However, the slight shift in emphasis from asking the Father in the Son's name to asking the Son directly was likely Jesus' intention. He is emphasizing to the disciples they will continue His works and greater ones still—in His absence (13:34,

---

35. The difficulty of this and the contrast between this form of prayer and what is typical (i.e., asking the Father in Jesus' name; cf. Matt 6:9) is seen in the split textual witnesses. See the additional note in Carson, *John*, 497, as well as footnote 73 in Ramsey, *John*, 781.

36; 14:2, etc.). Not yet understanding those works will be empowered by Christ's Spirit, He increases their confidence by giving the disciples more reason to pray for Jesus' assistance in those works—"I myself will do" them. I have made this even more emphatic by drawing out the inherent first-person singular pronoun from the verb, "to do."

This is slightly different than what Jesus said in verse 13. There, the focus was on a generic "whatever you all may ask in My name." The implication was the one being asked in the name of the Son was the Father.[36] Here it is different: Jesus encourages the disciples to ask saying not only will the Father hear and answer, but the Son will hear and "do" Himself.

## Conclusion

In John 14:12–14, Jesus promises the continuity of His works and the works of the ones who believe in Him who will follow Him. Our expectation is those works will not be archetypal but ectypal, that is, not new but according to the paradigm in use by the Lord Himself, the offices of prophet, priest, and king.

While the New Testament continues to expand on this principle (e.g., Eph 4:11–12, 1 Cor 12:4–11), it firmly establishes there are mediatorial works of the Lord that will not be continued and are, indeed, finished. As noted above, however, to assign the church His works and greater ones still does not do violence to Jesus' once-for-all work as our Mediator. Instead, John 14:12–14 establishes the groundwork for the continued ministry of the application of Christ's work in the church.

What would they do? Works of the same kind as His, namely, as prophets, priests, and kings. Would they continue in the same intensity and scope? No: they would be "greater still" than those He had done. Does this put the church's ministry on "equal" footing with the Lord's? No: to do the works of the Lord and greater

---

36. Ramsey, *John*, 781; Carson, *John*, 497; Borchert, *John 12–21*, 117.

## The Promise and Provision of "Greater Works"

ones still requires prayerful dependence upon Him, seeking power in His name. Köstenberger helpfully writes:

> Works done in the era subsequent to that of the earthly Jesus are greater, not because of the human being doing them but owing to Jesus' exalted position with the Father and to his complete authority, as well as on account of Jesus' answer of the disciples' prayers in his name and his sending of the Spirit as a helping presence for his followers."[37]

## SECTION 2: THE PROVISION OF GREATER WORKS: EPHESIANS 4:7-12

### Introduction

As we saw above, the Lord promised the disciples they would do the work He was doing and greater works still. He puts this in covenantal terms, that is, He Himself promises to do the works they request. This would begin immediately after Pentecost with the outpouring of the Holy Spirit on the assembled church. Strictly speaking, the provision for the church's greater works is the Holy Spirit. It is only by His indwelling and His work in the believer do we do the works the Lord explained.

In the next chapter, we will further investigate the role of the Holy Spirit as the necessary provision for the practice of greater works. In this present section, we are assuming that discussion in part because, in my view, Eph 4:7-12 provides a better starting point for understanding the church's work according to the offices of prophet, priest, and king.

Three further clarifying comments are needed. First, as we will see below (but especially in the next chapter), upon the Lord's ascension He gave to each believer a measure of the Spirit for the works He promised they would do, that is what we commonly call a "spiritual gift." In our text, specifically in verses 11-12, He gave gifts to some that would be the provision for the proper function

---

37. Köstenberger, "Greater Works of the Believer," 42.

of other spiritual gifts. It would not be correct to call these gifts more important.[38] Rather, the five[39] roles listed in our text are provided by the Lord to be the provision for the rest of the church. In other words, while the gifts listed in verse 11 are part of the overall endowment of the spiritual gifts illustrated in greater detail in other lists of gifts (e.g., Rom 12:6–8, 1 Cor 12:4–11, and 1 Pet 4:10–11), these stand in front of other gifts in order that those gifts may function properly.

Second, verse 12 explains the connection between the gifts listed in verse 11 and the rest of the gift lists in the New Testament. This is an extension of my previous point. For example, while 1 Cor 12:7 explains gifts are for the "common good," the rest of the passage does not explain how that is; our text deals with that omission. It explains the "equipping" function that allows the rest of the gifts to work properly. The epistles of the New Testament, then, unpack the endowment of the Spirit given to His disciples in manifold spiritual gifts.

Third, I will interact with this more below, but it is important also to follow the exegesis in seeing two things. First, it is true that some of the roles listed below (e.g., prophet) had foundational, non-repeating functions in the early church.[40] And yet, second, as we saw in our exegesis of John 14:12–14 above, in the church age, there will be functions and roles *analogous* to the foundational, apostolic ones. To assert this isn't to suggest the foundational role of apostle, for example, continues in the church. Rather, the functions of the apostle, or, apostle-like functions, may continue. If we fail to recognize these dynamics, we will not see how our paradigm applies to our context. A translation of our text is in Figure 1 below.

---

38. That would explicitly violate passages such as Rom 12:4–8 and 1 Cor 12:11, 18.

39. More on that decision below.

40. For example, the apostles Peter, James, John, or Paul. We can say this about the types in the Old Testament as well, e.g., Moses and Melchizedek.

## The Promise and Provision of "Greater Works"

| Verse | Line | |
|---|---|---|
| 7 | 1 | To each one of us was given the grace |
|   | 2 | According to a measure of the bounty from Christ |
| 8 | 3 | Therefore it says |
|   | 4 | When He ascended on high |
|   | 5 | He led a host of captives [and also] |
|   | 6 | He gave gifts to men |
| 9 | 7 | (When it says, 'He ascended' what is it but |
|   | 8 | He also descended |
|   | 9 | Into the lower parts of the earth? |
| 10 | 10 | The one descending, He is also the one who ascended |
|   | 11 | Far above all the heavens |
|   | 12 | That He might fill all things) |
| 11 | 13 | And, on the one hand, He gave |
|   | 14 | Apostles, on the other |
|   | 15 | Prophets, on the other |
|   | 16 | Evangelists, on the other |
|   | 17 | Shepherds and teachers |
| 12 | 18 | For the equipment of the saints |
|   | 19 | To the work of ministry [and] |
|   | 20 | To the building of the body of Christ |

**Figure 1.**

## Commentary

*Lines 1–2 (v.7). "To each one of us was given the grace according to a measure of the bounty from Christ."*

After the apostle urged the church to live in a manner commensurate with "the calling to which you have been called" (4:1), he explains it should take the shape of certain attitudes and actions (4:2). These maintain the oneness of the church wrought through the Holy Spirit (4:3–6; cf. 2:11–19). To that singular body, each one individually was given an endowment of grace. "To each one

Part Two | Typology Trajectory

of us" refers to each of the individuals who have been, by grace through faith evident in baptism (4:5), made members of the one body (4:4). He includes himself in the distribution.[41]

In light of the unity of the body, he speaks of its diversity in the apportionment of God's grace: individual "grace was given."[42] Charles Hodge comments, "This unity of the church, although it involves the essential equality of all believers, is still consistent with great diversity as to gifts, influence, and honor."[43] Christ is the giver of this grace, the church the recipients.[44]

Paul's use of "grace" in Ephesians is broad, and so the context must determine its definition beyond the non-contextual meaning, e.g., favor or kindness.[45] It is both the freely given inward-regenerating work of God (1:6–7; 2:5, 7–8) and the outward working in specific functions (3:2, 7–8; 4:7, 29).[46] Here, "grace" is used as a synonym for "gifts" He distributes to the church.[47] It is also used to describe those gifts, that they are evidences of Christ's favor and kindness to His people.[48]

To each one grace was given "according to a measure of the bounty from Christ." "According to a measure" is a phrase most likely of "measure."[49] It explains the extent of the sovereign distribution of grace (or gifts) in "measures," that is, as each one has need according to the Lord's will. This manner of distribution is clear in a similar Pauline passage, 1 Cor 12:11: "All these are

41. Arnold, *Ephesians*, 246; O'Brien, *Ephesians*, 287.

42. Fowl, *Ephesians*, 136.

43. Hodge, *Commentary on Ephesians*, 211. See also Vincent, *Word Studies in the New Testament*, 3:388.

44. Arnold rightly calls this a "divine passive," *Ephesians*, 246.

45. In the New Testament, this is expanded into: blessing (1), concession (1), credit (3), favor (11), gift (1), grace (122), gracious (2), gracious work (3), gratitude (1), thank (3), thankfulness (2), thanks (6). Thomas and Wilkins, *New American Standard Exhaustive Concordance of the Bible*.

46. These divide up in meaning following the classic Pauline division of the book: indicatives (chs. 1–3) and imperatives (chs. 4–6). Hodge, *Ephesians*, 211.

47. Arnold, *Ephesians*, 246.

48. The words translated "grace" and "gift" come from the same root. *LN*, 298.

49. Wallace, *Basics of New Testament Syntax*, 90.

empowered by one and the same Spirit, who apportions to each one individually as he wills." This grace flows out of the "bounty from Christ." "Bounty" is preferred over "gift" (e.g., ESV) as it derives from a different verb[50] and it allows a closer connection to the riches and generosity of Christ.

### Lines 3–6 (v.8). "Therefore it says, 'When He ascended on high He led a host of captives [and also] He gave gifts to men."

With this citation from Ps 68:18, Paul does two things. First, he draws on the original intent and meaning of Ps 68 and interprets the Psalm christologically. John Stott wrote, "Paul applies this picture to Christ's ascension not arbitrarily because he detected a vague analogy between the two but justifiably because he saw in the exaltation of Jesus a further fulfillment of this description of the triumph of God."[51] The Divine Warrior of Ps 68 is the Lord Jesus. "On high" was the mount of God (Ps 68:16), Zion, the place of the Temple. For the apostle Paul, "on high" is "far above all the heavens" (4:10). The warrior's ascent to the throne in victory is the Lord's ascent into the heavens in victory.

In so doing, two things happened. First, in "He led a host of captives," he highlights the victory of Christ over the principalities and powers (cf. Col 2:15).[52] John Calvin saw in Ps 68 a typical song of triumph of God over His enemies in which He was victorious for His people. He wrote, "But no ascension of God more triumphant or memorable will ever occur, than that which took place when Christ was carried up the right hand of the Father that he

---

50. These are related verbs to be sure but the context calls for a slightly different translation. From "doreōmai" 'to give, to grant,' rather than "dĭdomi" to give an object," LN, 565–566.

51. Stott, *Message of Ephesians*, 156–57.

52. O'Brien, *Ephesians*, 289; Hodge, *Ephesians*, 213–214; Osborne, *Ephesians: Verse by Verse*, 121. Sproul sees these captives as "Christ's people whom Christ defeated in the sense of destroying their sins and setting them free," Sproul, *Purpose of God*, 102.

## Part Two | Typology Trajectory

might rule over all authorities and power and might become the everlasting guardian and protector of his people."[53]

Secondly, the divine warrior received gifts from His people as a result of His victory (Ps 68:18b). Here, Paul interprets that victory as foreshadowing the gracious victorious Christ who, instead of receiving gifts from His people, gives gifts to them as a result of His victory.[54] I am sympathetic with R. C. Sproul who wrote, "After Jesus ascended into heaven in triumph and sat at the right hand of God, perhaps the first act of the new King was Pentecost (Acts 2), when he poured out his Holy Spirit to gift every member of his church."[55]

*Lines 7–12 (vv.9–10). "When it says, 'He ascended' what is it but He also descended to the lower parts of the earth? The one descending, He is also the one who ascended far above all the heavens that He might fill all things."*

Among the issues commentators note in this verse are:

a. To what is the descent referring?

b. What are the "lower parts of the earth"?

c. What about the inclusion of "first" in some of the old manuscripts, namely, "He also first descended..."?[56]

---

53. Calvin, *Commentary on the Epistle of Paul the Apostle to the Ephesians*, 272.

54. The extended discussions in O'Brien, *Letter to the Ephesians*, 289–293, and Arnold, *Ephesians*, 247–252, summarize the interpretative challenges in Paul's apparent reversal of "receiving" to "giving." I believe Arnold's conclusion that Paul was aware of both the Hebrew and LXX of Ps 68 but chose "to bring out the full meaning of the text of Psalm 68 by simply not citing it verbatim" (along with his other stated lines of proof) is persuasive. Stott says simply, "What conquerors took from their captives, they gave away to their own people." Stott, *Ephesians*,157.

55. Sproul, *Ephesians*, 102.

56. For our purposes, adjudication of these issues is not germane. I would call attention to the discussion in Arnold, 252–254, O'Brien, 293–297, Hodge, 219–222, or Osborne, 123–125.

## The Promise and Provision of "Greater Works"

For our purposes, the implication of Paul's use of Ps 68 is to show it is the Risen Christ who is giving grace (gifts) to His people. While 1 Cor 12 makes it clear the distribution of gifts is superintended by the Spirit, here, Paul's focus is on Christ's apportionment from the bounty of His victory.[57]

*Lines 13-17 (v.11). "And, on the one hand, He gave apostles; on the other, prophets; on the other, evangelists; on the other, shepherds and teachers."*

In this verse, Paul returns to the argument he introduced in verse 7. There he explained to each was given a measure of grace, that is, a gift to an individual. That measured distribution matters as here, he opens with "And, on the one hand, He gave." "He gave" uses the same subject-verb arrangement as we saw in verse 7 (the divine passive) and the second part of verse 8 ("He gave gifts to men"): as before, here the Lord is the giver.

Of the verb "gave," Wallace indicates "*past* time with reference to the time of speaking."[58] Here the verb means the Lord began an action. When Paul described the Lord's action (the giving of gifts), in the use of this verb, he subtly indicated the giving had passed (in one sense that is true since Pentecost was history at the time of the writing). But, the giving has not passed since the Spirit continues to give gifts to those He regenerates. The verb (an aorist) handles both senses. In terms of the work and greater works, this inaugurated era we call the "era of ectypes."

This assertion, that we are in the "era of ectypes" depends upon our exegesis of John 14:12-14. As we noted there, Jesus promised the church would be empowered to do His work and greater works. Jesus did His work according to the offices of prophet, priest, and king, and, as we'll show below, the gifting

---

57. O'Brien, *Ephesians*, 297. Arnold writes, "In the exercise of his ruling sovereignty at the right hand of God, Christ is now unfolding a comprehensive plan for the universe," Arnold, *Ephesians*, 255.

58. Wallace, *Basics of New Testament Syntax*, 239, italics in original.

listed in the New Testament indicates the passing through of these offices is how to understand the gifts of the Holy Spirit.

Paul gives five leading examples. As I said above, while none of these gifts is inherently more Spirit-given and Spirit-directed than another, these stand ahead of the other gifts as they provide for the proper functioning of the rest of the gifts. I believe O'Brien is correct when he says these have a "foundational role as the authoritative recipients and proclaimers of the mystery of Christ."[59] As my analysis below will show of some gifts, their presence would not survive the death of the last apostle. But of others, they would be in the founding era of the church and last until the Lord returns.[60]

Paul makes his list illustrative by using the particle construction, "on the one hand ... on the other."[61] As I have translated it, it reads, "On the one hand, He gave apostles; on the other, prophets" and so on. The implication is that some were given these roles as their measure of grace and others were not; they were gifted differently.[62] In calling this era the "era of ectypes" we should understand Paul is detailing some of the roles and functions of those who would be carrying on the work of Christ as prophets, priests, and kings. In the rest of the New Testament, it is the purpose of the Holy Spirit to use other descriptive words to describe the ministry of the ectypes.[63]

"Apostle." This word, *apostolos*, is the noun form of the verb "to send" transliterated right from the Greek. It means "sent one" or "messenger." In the New Testament, it is defined in three ways. First, in its general form, all those who are sent of the Lord are

---

59. O'Brien, *Ephesians*, 298. Sinclair Ferguson perhaps goes further when speaking the apostles, prophets and evangelists, "These callings belong to the inaugural life of the New Testament church." Ferguson, *Let's Study Ephesians*, 107.

60. I would make further qualification when it comes to the so-called "miraculous gifts" of speaking / interpreting in tongues, miracles and healing. More details on this point will be provided in the next chapter.

61. Liddell, *Lexicon*, 498.

62. Stott, *Ephesians*, 160.

63. E.g., Rom 12, 1 Cor 12 and 1 Pet 4.

## The Promise and Provision of "Greater Works"

"apostles." Jesus uses it this way in John 13:16: "Truly, truly, I say to you, a servant is not greater than his master, nor is a messenger (*apostolos*) greater than the one who sent him."[64] Second, the word is used is to denote the ones who were chosen by the Lord as direct witnesses of His ministry. Peter defined it this way in Acts 1:21–23, "So one of the men who have accompanied us during all the time that the Lord Jesus went in and out among us, beginning from the baptism of John until the day when he was taken up from us—one of these men must become with us a witness (*apostolos*) to his resurrection."[65] A third way is how Paul uses this word to describe himself (e.g., Eph 1:1) and those who are sent out as messengers (*apostolos*) of the churches (2 Cor 8:23; cf. Acts 14:14).[66]

Of which three definitions does Paul mean here? The immediate context is of little help. Arnold writes, "Christ is continuing to give these leaders to the church for the equipping of individual members and facilitating their growth to maturity."[67] Osborne agrees with Arnold and doesn't see the New Testament supporting the end of the gift of apostle.[68] Hodge believes the gift of apostle perished with the last man who had seen the Lord and was commissioned as a result.[69] Sproul agrees with Hodge.[70] Peter O'Brien, however, thinks the cessation view is "unnecessary."[71]

We can be helped by remembering the gift of "apostle" is an ec-type of Christ. That is, an apostle is one who is sent from Christ just as the Lord Jesus was sent by the Father (e.g., John 6:57). The Father's sending of Christ meant He did unique, unrepeatable apostolic

---

64. See also John 17:18, 20:21 for the verb forms.

65. BAGD has all three definitions under *apostolos*, 99.

66. He uses it to describe Epaphroditus in Phil 2:25 and in this way we can see an example of this gift in the local church. It is also true, however, that Paul as an apostle was himself numbered among the twelve according to Peter's definition in Acts 1.

67. Arnold, *Ephesians*, 256.

68. Osborne, *Ephesians*, 126.

69. Hodge, *Ephesians*, 223.

70. Sproul, *Ephesians*, 102.

71. O'Brien, *Ephesians*, 298.

## Part Two | Typology Trajectory

work, e.g., established the inbreaking of the kingdom once for all (Mark 1:15). However, as the sent one, Christ also established a pattern of kingdom inbreaking taken up by those He initially chose (the Twelve: Matt 10:5), a larger group He chose (the seventy-two: Luke 10:1) and then an even larger group (Acts 10:44–48).

The Lord Jesus as the archetype meant there were foundational aspects of His work as God's sent one that were not to be repeated. The same is true concerning the gift of apostle in the early church: using the Acts 1:21–23 definition, there are no more apostles in the church. What they did was build a foundation for the household of God founded upon Christ Jesus the cornerstone (Eph 2:19–20) that was not to be laid again. While this unique aspect of the apostles' work is complete, no one would say the same about the "messenger mission" of Matt 28:19–20. Thought of as ectypal work, there is nothing in the New Testament to suggest Jesus no longer sends messengers who start churches to see people saved from their sins and built up in the faith.

"Prophet." The prophets (prophētēs) were historically chosen by God to receive direct revelation from Him to deliver to the people of God.[72] Moses is the primary type in this regard (cf. Deuteronomy 18:15).[73] Jesus, also, as the archetype, is God's prophet (cf. Luke 4:18–19). The Old Testament prophets up through John the Baptist as well as the Lord Jesus, received direct, infallible revelation from God and delivered it to the people.[74] John Stott is correct when he writes, "In this sense we must again insist that there are no prophets today."[75]

After the Lord Jesus as the archetype there are now prophetic ectypes. Paul refers to one category of prophets of this type in Eph 3:4–5: "When you read this, you can perceive my insight into the mystery of Christ which was not made known to the sons of men in other generations as it has now been revealed to his holy

---

72. Grudem defines them as those "telling something that God has spontaneously brought to mind" Grudem, *Systematic Theology*, 1049.

73. Paul refers to these prophets also in Rom 1:2 and 3:21.

74. E.g., Matt 14:5.

75. Stott, *Ephesians*, 161.

## The Promise and Provision of "Greater Works"

apostles and prophets (prophētēs ) by the Spirit." As in Eph 2:20, the Lord selected prophets who had an unrepeatable ministry of delivering God's word to the church so that once completed, the church can be "built together into a dwelling place for God by the Spirit" (2:22b).

However, the apostle Paul explains to the Corinthian church, there is another kind of prophet whose role is to speak to "people for the upbuilding and encouragement and consolation" (1 Cor 14:3). That is another prophetic ectype. If we understand the apostle Paul as a prophet (in the sense of Eph 2:20, 3:5), his Corinthian correspondence is providing for them the source material so the prophets to whom he refers in 14:3 can provide "upbuilding," "encouragement," and "consolation" to the church. The prophets referred to in 14:3 are prophets not in receiving new words from the Lord but in taking God's revealed word and preaching, teaching and counseling it in the lives of the church.[76] Those gifted by the Spirit to continue this work are prophetic ectypes.

"Evangelist." The third foundational role the Lord gave to the church were "the evangelists" (euaggelistēs). The word itself simply means "preacher of the gospel."[77] If Paul intended some kind of priority in this list, with the evangelists it may be he concerns himself more intently with those gifts that would endure until Christ's return. Beyond its appearance here, the New Testament uses this term in only two places. Once to describe Philip the deacon (Acts 21:8) and once to exhort Timothy to "do the work of an evangelist" (2 Tim 4:5).

Two different possible evangelistic ministries are represented by these two cases. The first with Philip, is itinerant, traveling evangelism (Acts 8:5 in Samaria; Acts 8:26–40 with the Ethiopian eunuch on the road to Gaza). The second possible evangelism ministry is with Timothy at Ephesus. His ministry, according to

---

76. John Stott tries to unpack what this gift might be. The options he sees: "a special gift of biblical exposition" or "a sensitive understanding of the contemporary world," along with an "indignant denunciation of the social sins of the day" or ones to "bring conviction of sin." These sound like biblical preachers! Stott, *Ephesians*, 162.

77. *BAGD*, 318.

## Part Two | Typology Trajectory

O'Brien is settled, pastoral ministry.[78] In the two letters addressed to Timothy, the apostle Paul gives to him a wide range of ministry exhortations, that he charge members to stay clear of different doctrines (1 Tim 1:3), urge members to prayer (2:1, 8), approve elder and deacon candidates (3:1–13), exhort and teach the church (4:13; 2 Tim 2:2, 24), and preach (4:2). It is in this last context where he is exhorted to do the work of an evangelist. It appears his evangelistic ministry was to be a normal part of the rest of his pastoral ministry. And, while there is no scriptural reason to regard itinerant evangelism to have ceased with the apostles, there certainly isn't warrant to assume evangelism as a ministry no longer belongs to the church.

Yet, it may still be challenging to distinguish between this role and the role of the apostle. Arnold draws the line by stating the evangelists were likely those who stayed behind once the apostles planted and established the churches.[79] This supports our view of Timothy's ministry. As the office of founding apostle passed from the scene, it may also be the apostolic role of planting and growing churches is most properly found to be the job of the evangelist.[80] Additionally, this gift (however it is understood) does not absolve members of churches from the work of sharing the gospel (cf. Matthew 28:19–20). For this reason, we are still on solid ground to consider the ectypal work of an evangelist not just at the foundation of the New Testament church but also as an enduring ectype of Christ's prophetic office.[81]

"Shepherds and teachers." These last two substantives complete the list of five foundational roles in the church. Paul's use of "shepherds [or "pastors"[82]] and teachers" (*poimēn* and *didas-*

---

78. O'Brien, *Ephesians*, 299.

79. Arnold, Ephesians, 259.

80. O'Brien, *Ephesians*, 29. In the Book of Church Order of the Presbyterian Church in America, 21–11, ordination to gospel ministry can be done as an "evangelist" if the charge is not to a particular (established) church but to a region for the purpose of establishing a church.

81. Stott, *Ephesians*, 163.

82. ESV, NASB, NIV, KJV all use "pastors."

## The Promise and Provision of "Greater Works"

kalos) has presented challenges to interpreters. First, the word for "shepherd" is rare in the New Testament, used only here to describe church leaders.[83] What it means to be a "shepherd" (pastor) must be deduced from other contexts. It is used to describe the Lord Jesus (Heb 13:20, 1 Pet 2:25), and it is how Jesus referred to Himself in John 10:11, 14. Deducing some of the shepherd / pastor's role from how He conducted Himself with His disciples is probably appropriate.[84] Some of what constitutes the role of a shepherd could be deduced from Jesus' exhortations to Peter in John 21:

> [15]When they had finished breakfast, Jesus said to Simon Peter, "Simon, son of John, do you love me more than these?" He said to him, "Yes, Lord; you know that I love you." He said to him, "Feed my lambs." [16]He said to him a second time, "Simon, son of John, do you love me?" He said to him, "Yes, Lord; you know that I love you." He said to him, "Tend my sheep." [17]He said to him the third time, "Simon, son of John, do you love me?" Peter was grieved because he said to him the third time, "Do you love me?" and he said to him, "Lord, you know everything; you know that I love you." Jesus said to him, "Feed my sheep.

"Feed My lambs . . .Tend My sheep . . .Feed My sheep." In these commands, Carson believes the Lord is giving to Peter (and subsequently to other shepherds) the opportunity to demonstrate love for the Lord by being a pastor of His people.[85]

Though Paul applies it uniquely in our text, he commanded the Ephesian elders to fill the role of shepherds over their flock, "Keep watch over yourselves and all the flock of which the Holy Spirit made you overseers" (Acts 20:28-29). In this case, Paul effectively called overseers "shepherds" (or "pastors").[86] At this point,

---

83. Arnold, *Ephesians*, 260.

84. For example, calling people to follow (Matt 4:18ff), teaching them (Matt 5-7), preaching (Matt 11:1) or praying (Matt 26:36).

85. Carson, *John*, 678. "That "shepherding" became a dominant metaphor for pastoral care is evident already within the New Testament," Ramsey, *John*, 1044-45.

86. Ferguson, *Ephesians*, 107-108.

using 1 Tim 3 and Titus 1, we could expand the job description of the shepherd or pastor to the church until Christ's return.

Secondly, these are also grammatically different from the rest of the roles listed in Eph 4:11. There the definite article appears ("the") before each of the other roles but here is found only before "shepherd." With its absence before "teacher," some believe Paul was speaking of only one role, i.e., "shepherd-teacher." There are differences of opinion about this among commentators. Some hold to one role.[87]

One argument marshalled in support of one role is a certain understanding of the Granville Sharp rule. The rule states, "When the [New Testament] construction article-substantive-kai-substantive (TSKS) involved personal nouns which were singular and not proper names, they always referred to the same person." Daniel Wallace, in his Greek grammar, explains Sharp's rule does not apply to two coordinated plural substantives (such as we have in our text). In our text "shepherds and teachers" does not clearly fit the criteria. So any appeal to the Sharp rule, and thus to one role on grammatical grounds, is mistaken.[88] Additionally, the presence of significantly overlapping responsibilities has led some to consider them a single role. While Calvin respects the views of Chrysostom and Augustine who hold they are the same role, he writes, "This does not appear to me a sufficient reason why the two offices, which I find to differ from each other, should be confounded."[89]

"Teachers" translates a common word (*didaskalos*) in the New Testament. In the list, they are grammatically distinct from the shepherds though their function is pastoral. Osborne defines their role, "'Teachers' are those who explain the truths of Christ to the people and lead them into the deep things of God and his word."[90] Teachers transmit sound doctrine (e.g., 1 Tim 1:10, 2 Tim

---

87. Sproul held this view, *Ephesians*, 102. As did Hodge, *Ephesians*, 227. Ferguson believes this might be the case, *Ephesians*, 107. Arnold (who does not hold this view) summarizes the commentators who do, *Ephesians*, 260.

88. Wallace, *Greek*, 270–290, esp. 284.

89. Calvin, *Ephesians*, 280.

90. Osborne, *Ephesians*, 127–28.

## The Promise and Provision of "Greater Works"

4:3) passing on apostolic tradition (2 Tim 2:2) to the churches. Shepherds (pastors) do the same, in fact, it is a qualification of the elders that they be able to teach (1 Tim 3:2). However, holding the two offices distinct means all pastors will be teachers, but only some teachers will be pastors.[91]

### Lines 18–20 (v.12). "For the equipment of the saints, to the work of ministry [and] to the building of the body of Christ."

In this verse, Paul gives the purpose for which the risen Christ has given these foundational gifts to the church: the equipping of the church for ministry. There are two questions to answer here. First, how is the substantive "equipment" to be rendered? Second, does the structure of the verse with its three prepositional phrases unpack the work of the five roles alone ("clerical" view) or do the five roles "equip" the church for these various work of ministry ("equipped priesthood of believers" view)?[92]

This substantive, "equipment," appears only here in the New Testament. Its root verb, while not appearing in the New Testament, oversees a family of terms that are variously translated as, for example, "mending" (Matt 4:21), "trained" (Luke 6:40), "prepared" (Rom 9:22), "arranged" (2 Cor 9:5) or "restored" (1 Pet 5:10). It is perhaps for this reason the substantive in this verse is rendered in two main ways. First as "equipping" (ESV), "training" (HCSB), or "prepare" (NIV). Or, second as "perfecting" (KJV, RSV). I believe it should be translated as "for the equipment" (largely similar to the ESV, "equipping") for the following reasons.[93]

It might first be said without reference to the context, God has always supplied His people with leaders who equipped them to be skilled in understanding the Lord and the world. God Himself first taught Adam with the expectation that he would equip his family. Subsequently, God provided prophets and priests in Israel

---

91. Ferguson, *Ephesians*, 107–108; Stott, *Ephesians*, 163–164.

92. Arnold, *Ephesians*, 262.

93. Notably, *BAGD* translated this "Equipping, equipment for something," 418.

who were types of Christ and His prophetic ministry.[94] Equipping the church has always been needed.

Exegetically, Eph 4:1–6 is Paul's call to the church to live a certain way, that is, displaying the fruit of the Spirit (4:2–3) in the context of the one confessing body (4:4–6). It is for this reason Paul exhorts Titus to train and appoint elders in the churches (Titus 1:5; see also 1 Tim 3:2). Relatedly, verses 13–15 picture the church in an environment of competing ideas and viewpoints (see also Col 2:4, 8). These verses definitely picture a need for training and leadership into maturity based on a right understanding of the faith. Arnold surveys the ways the related verb is translated in the New Testament and finds the closest parallel to Paul's usage in 2 Tim 3:16–17: "All Scripture is breathed out by God and profitable for teaching, for reproof, for correction, and for training in righteousness, that the man of God may be complete, equipped[95] for every good work." Here the man of God is equipped for every good work and not "perfected" for every good work.[96]

The second question needing an answer regards the structure of the verse. Paul's use of prepositional phrases has led to differing opinions on the logic of the verse, namely, is he advocating a more "clerical" view (e.g., these are specific, ordained clergy roles) or a "priesthood of believers" view?[97] As I have shown in Figure 1 above, I believe they are structured as follows:

> For the equipment of the saints
>
> To the work of ministry [and]
>
> To the building of the body of Christ[98]

---

94. Calvin, *Ephesians*, 282.

95. Meaning to make someone completely adequate or sufficient for something—'to make adequate, to furnish completely, to cause to be fully qualified, adequacy.' *LN*, 679.

96. Arnold, *Ephesians*, 263.

97. By "clerical" I mean a sharper focus on the ministry of ordained officers. T. David Gordon holds such a view, Gordon, "'Equipping' Ministry in Ephesians 4?"

98. This is the same structure in Arnold, *Ephesians*, 262; Stott, *Ephesians*, 166–168.

## The Promise and Provision of "Greater Works"

I believe the five roles are the implied subjects of the first phrase while the church is the subject of the last two. In other words, I hold to the equipped "priesthood of believers" view. While most commentators agree with both an equipping church leadership and an actively ministering congregation, this may not be a meaningful difference though I will show below that I believe it is.[99]

I hold this view for two main reasons. First, while these three prepositional phrases share a similar structure[100] there are reasons not to take these phrases as coordinate phrases. The change in preposition from *pros* to *eis* from the first phrase to the remaining, may signal subordinate structure.[101] If the apostle Paul intended for these three phrases to be coordinate, why did he choose a different preposition for the first? Though the unaffected meanings of these are close, Paul uses distinct words.[102] While O'Brien asserts it may be too much to ask of the prepositions themselves, if there is movement in Paul's argument, namely from the work of the five roles (4:11) to all of God's people (cf. "saints" in 4:12), then a change in preposition would make sense.[103] Osborne agrees, due to the use of the different prepositions, "Paul is probably intentional in making the second and third subordinate to the first."[104]

The second reason I believe Paul intends the last two prepositional phrases to be subordinate to the first has to do with the

---

99. Calvin doesn't mention it, *Ephesians*, 281–282; Ferguson isn't sure it is, *Ephesians*, 110. I would say the same about Hendriksen, *Galatians, Ephesians, Philippians, Colossians, and Philemon*, 198. Hodge admits variations, "The word, katartismōs rendered *perfecting*, admits of different interpretations," *Ephesians*, 227–228. T. David Gordon, however, believes strongly in the difference adopting the former clerical view.

100. An accusative preposition + genitive object.

101. Arnold admits this is the only occurrence of this prepositional pattern in the NT and then argues for this point by calling attention to usage in the LXX where the first phrase is not coordinate with ones that follow, *Ephesians*, 262.

102. Wallace, *Greek Grammar*, 369, 380.

103. O'Brien, *Ephesians*, 302–303.

104. Osborne, *Ephesians*, 128. Gordon admits there might be further discussion about Paul's differing use of prepositions, he believes these prepositions are interchangeable and therefore can't signal anything but coordinate structure, Gordon, "'Equipping' Ministry in Ephesians 4?," 72.

object of "equipment," namely "the saints." As I mentioned above, Paul's address changes from the five roles of 4:11 to the overall church in 4:12, "saints." If Paul had only the five roles in mind for the entire text, it is hard to see why he would've introduced the broader church in verse 12. Two other minor notes of difference are that, first, the object of this preposition is articular while the other prepositions' object are not and, second, "the saints" is an objective genitive while the remaining genitives vary (genitives of apposition and object, respectively).

The ascended Christ gives the church the five roles so that they would equip the saints in the congregation in two related ways: "to the works of ministry" and "to the building up of the body of Christ." The "works of ministry"[105] are those good works the Lord has created all the saints (4:7, 16; 1 Corinthians 12:7) to walk in (cf. 2:10). O'Brien writes, "Christ has given 'special' ministers so that they 'make God's people fully qualified,' thus enabling them to serve their Lord by serving one another."[106]

The saints are equipped for ministry and that is its own end though it isn't the only end. That ministry will result in the steady "building up of the body of Christ." "Building up" the body of Christ is a common Pauline theme.[107] The word group involves construction. Used in a spiritual sense (as it is here), it means spiritual strengthening, edifying, building up.[108] We know from the rest of the pericope that includes:

> [13]...until we all attain to the unity of the faith and of the knowledge of the Son of God, to mature manhood, to the measure of the stature of the fullness of Christ, [14]so that we may no longer be children, tossed to and fro by the waves and carried about by every wind of doctrine, by human cunning, by craftiness in deceitful schemes.

---

105. Genitive of apposition, "works, namely, ministry," Wallace, *Greek Grammar*, 95.
106. O'Brien, *Ephesians*, 303, citing *LN*, 679.
107. Found 15 times in Paul's letters.
108. *BAGD*, 559.

*The Promise and Provision of "Greater Works"*

¹⁵Rather, speaking the truth in love, we are to grow up in every way into him who is the head, into Christ.

## Conclusion

In this section, we have considered Eph 4:7–12 and the role this text plays in unpacking the provision of the greater works in the church. John 14 introduced Jesus' promise of greater works, and here, how He provides for the church so that we will do them. Endowed by the Holy Spirit, these five roles stand ahead of the other gifts ensuring that their practice will be according to the Scriptures and hitting its mark, namely, works of ministry unto the building up of the body of Christ.

The apostles and prophets clearly had foundational and non-repeatable roles in establishing the post-Pentecost church. At the same time, these roles (informed by other texts in the New Testament) are repeated in the church though wisdom might dictate not calling them "Apostle" or "Prophet"! Evangelists, shepherds (pastors), and teachers also provided an essential foundational role as the church began, yet it is easier to understand how these roles were never intended to end at the end of the apostolic age.

## THE PROMISE AND THE PROVISION OF GREATER WORKS: CONCLUSION

We have followed the logic of the Lord's promise of greater works and the provision for doing them. The former was found in John 14:12–14. There, Jesus explained to His disciples that He was transitioning out of His works and passing on to them their ministry of applying that work to the nations.

"Greater" works than the Lord's meant the application of His ministry of reconciliation done by the power of the Holy Spirit under His Headship until He returns. While there is significant continuity in the works of the disciples and that of the Lord, the

## Part Two | Typology Trajectory

disciples' works would be greater in scope, greater in impact and greater in number as they are done in a greater age, the Eschaton.

The provision for these greater works is the Holy Spirit. Yet the Holy Spirit works mediately through the gifting He gives to the church in its members. That gifting has structure. First, that structure included some gifts acting at the inauguration of the post-Pentecost church mainly in the apostles and prophets. While there are no more apostles (that is, those directly and personally chosen by the Lord and sent on the mission), the apostolic ministry, the "messenger ministry" of Matt 28:18–20 endures. Indeed, there are no men receiving direct revelation of the Lord as the foundational New Testament prophets did, but now the prophetic ministry is in teaching and applying the Word of God revealed in the Scriptures. This is preeminently done in the preaching of the gospel. Finally, the ministries of evangelist, pastor and teacher set the course for the young church and carry her to Christ's return through the ministry of word and sacrament.

In the next chapter, we will more closely consider the Holy Spirit's work in more broadly gifting the church, that is, we will investigate the practice of greater works in the local church through the prophetic, priestly, and kingly ectypes.

# PART THREE

*The Paradigm in Action*

# CHAPTER FIVE

## The Practice of "Greater Works"

IN THE PREVIOUS TWO chapters, we investigated the biblical data concerning the typological framework of the three-fold office of Christ as our Mediator: prophet, priest, and king. After considering the Old Testament "types" of Christ and the fulfillment of those shadows by Christ Himself as the Archetype, we began considering the meaning of Jesus' words in John 14:12-14. In that text, we summarized Jesus' words as the "promise" of greater works. Although His work of redemption is complete, its application to the elect of all nations and ages remains.

Therefore, we needed to further explore how the church would do these greater works, so we turned to the next logical step in that process looking to Eph 4:7-11. We considered it before looking to other places in the New Testament where spiritual gifts are mentioned as it logically precedes those texts speaking of Christ giving gifts at His ascension rather than the Holy Spirit giving them in His Pentecostal descent.[1] There we have the "provision" of greater works in the foundational roles specifically in verses 11-12: "And [Christ] gave the apostles, the prophets, the evangelists, the shepherds and teachers, to equip the saints for the work of ministry, for building up the body of Christ."

---

1. Though there may not be any meaningful temporal difference in these events. It seemed more logical to consider them as we have.

Part Three | The Paradigm in Action

What has been lacking in our study thus far is the due consideration of the Holy Spirit as the Provision empowering both the foundational roles of apostle, prophet, etc. as well as the roles and gifts listed in the New Testament. Therefore, in this final doctrinal chapter we will consider the ministry of the Holy Spirit in the "practice" of greater works in three steps. First, we will briefly consider the person and work of the Holy Spirit to establish His role as the true provision. Second, we will briefly consider "spiritual gifts" as a doctrinal topic. Lastly, we will survey the gift lists in the New Testament and appropriately group them according to the prophet, priest, and king framework.

## SECTION 1: THE PROVISION FOR THE PRACTICE OF GREATER WORKS: THE HOLY SPIRIT

### The Person of the Holy Spirit

An inseparable connection exists between the work of the Son and the continuation of His work by the Holy Spirit.[2] For the Son to leave with His work incomplete (i.e., John 14:12) meant another like Him would have to come in His place; indeed, He promised that it would be so. In other words, for the church's full provision to do the greater works of the Son, the One who comes in the Son's name must be like the Son, both a Person and God. A brief theology of the person of the Spirit is following in three headings: activity, personhood, and God.

*Active.*

Like the Son, the Holy Spirit is active. The terms used to describe the Holy Spirit (*ruach* in Hebrew) and (*pneuma* in Greek) have unaffected definitions of "wind."[3] J. I. Packer lists seven different ways the Holy Spirit is active in the Old Testament. He:

  2. See, for example, John 14:16-18.
  3. Owen, *Holy Spirit*, 6. See also *BAGD*, 674. Also Brown, et al., *Hebrew and English Lexicon*, 924.

## The Practice of "Greater Works"

- Molds creation (Gen 1:2)
- Controls the course of history (Ps 104:29–30)
- Reveals God's truth (e.g., Num 24:2)
- Teaches God's people the way of faithfulness (Neh 9:20)
- Elicits personal responses to God (Ps 51:10–12)
- Equips individuals for leadership (Gen 41:38)
- Equips individuals with skills (Exod 31:1–11).

Packer summarizes these actions of the Spirit as "creator, controller, revealer, quickener, and enabler."[4]

*Person.*

More than simply being active, like the Son, the Holy Spirit is a person. The Bible attributes different personal characteristics to the Spirit.[5] I will mention four. First, according to the biblical data, He is a distinct person from the Father and the Son. For example, He alone hovered over the waters (Gen 1:2; cf. Ps 33:6), He is one of three who commissions (Matthew 28:19), He saves whomever He wills (John 3:5–8), He is sent from the Father (John 14:26), and He is sent from the Son (John 16:7; 20:22).[6]

Second, He is "another" Helper in the stead of the Lord Jesus. In John 14:16 (v. 26; 15:26, 16:7), Jesus says, "And I will ask the Father and he will give you another Helper, to be with you

---

4. Packer, *Keep in Step with the Spirit*, 52. A sampling of New Testament passages in further support of the Spirit's active ministry includes: conceiving the Messiah in Mary (Matt 1:18); ordaining Him (Matt 3:16); giving life (John 6:63); guiding the church (John 16:13); indwelling the elect (e.g., Acts 2:4); directing the ministers (Acts 8:29, 15:28); interceding for the church (Rom 8:26); giving gifts to the church (1 Cor 12:7); teaching (1 Tim 4:1) and giving the final invitation to our eternal rest (Rev 22:17).

5. Owen, *Holy Spirit*, 7; Winslow, *Work of the Holy Spirit*, 13–21; Fee, *God's Empowering Presence*, 829–31.

6. Vaughan, *Gifts of the Holy Spirit*, 403–15.

forever."[7] On the one hand, in speaking this way, the Lord reveals the Spirit whom He will send will not be unlike Him (e.g., *heteros*) but another (*allos*). But also, like Him the Spirit will be "with you" (e.g., John 14:9, ". . . Jesus said to him, "Have I been with you so long, and you still do not know me, Philip?").

Third, the Bible describes the Spirit using personal pronouns (e.g., I, me, he). For example in Acts 13:2, "While they were worshipping the Lord and fasting, the Holy Spirit said, 'Set apart for Me, Barnabas and Saul for the work to which I have called them.'" Also, Jesus makes note of this in John 15:26, "But when the Helper comes, whom I will send to you from the Father the Spirit of truth, who proceeds from the Father, He will bear witness about Me."[8]

Fourth, the Bible teaches the Spirit does what people do: He is grieved (Isa 63:10; Eph 4:30), He teaches (John 14:26), He bears witness (John 15:26; Rom 8:16), He prays (Rom 8:26–27), He searches God (1 Cor 2:10), He knows God (1 Cor 2:11), He forbids certain activities (Acts 16:6–7), He speaks (Acts 8:29; 13:2), He approves (Acts 15:28), He helps (Rom 8:14, 26), and He leads (Gal 5:18).[9] A. W. Pink writes, "Such is the Holy Spirit: all the elements which constitute personality are ascribed to and found in Him."[10]

## God.

The Holy Spirit is an active Person and He is also God. Packer says that by calling the Spirit "holy" He is, by definition, God.[11] There are many scriptural proofs for the deity of the Spirit.[12]

---

7. Packer, *Keep in Step with the Spirit*, 54.

8. See also John 14:16–17, 26, 16:8, 13, 14.

9. Pink, *Holy Spirit*, 12–14.

10. Pink, *Holy Spirit*, 12.

11. Packer, *Keep in Step with the Spirit*, 54. See also Louis Berkhof, *Systematic Theology*, 97–98.

12. Winslow lists the following with scriptural proofs, the Spirit is eternal, omniscient, omnipotent, omnipresent and sovereign; *Work of the Holy Spirit*, 21–22. See also Owen, *Holy Spirit*, 7–8.

## The Practice of "Greater Works"

- The divine equalities where the Father, Son and Spirit are set together as God[13]
- Whatever God calls His "temple" is where He dwells. 1 Cor 3:16, 6:19:

    "Do you not know that you are God's temple and that God's Spirit dwells in you? . . . Or do you not know that your body is a temple of the Holy Spirit within you whom you have from God?"

    Ephesians 2:22, "In Him you also are being built together into a dwelling place for God by the Spirit."

- In John 14:16, 18, Jesus talks about another Helper who is the Spirit by whom He will come to them:

    "And I will ask the Father and he will give you another Helper to be with you forever, even the Spirit of truth . . . I will not leave you as orphans; I will come to you."

- The omnipresence of the Holy Spirit, namely, the Spirit as God, is at all places at all times. In Ps 139:7–8 the parallelism indicates the deity of the Spirit:

    "Where shall I go from Your Spirit? Or where shall I flee from Your presence?"

- Fifth, the omniscience of the Holy Spirit seen in 1 Cor 2:10–11:

    "These things God has revealed to us through the Spirit. For the Spirit searches everything, even the depths of God."

- Lastly, the Bible teaches that to sin against the Holy Spirit is to sin against God. Acts 5:3–4:

    "But Peter said, "Ananias, why has Satan filled your heart to lie to the Holy Spirit and to keep back for yourself part of the proceeds of the land? While it remained unsold,

---

13. Matt 28:19; 1 Cor 12:4–6; 2 Cor 13:14; Eph 4:4–6; 1 Pet 1:2; Jude 20–21.

did it not remain your own? And after it was sold, was it not at your disposal? Why is it that you have contrived this deed in your heart? You have not lied to man but to God."[14]

The person of the Holy Spirit, is handsomely summarized in articles 5–11 of the Athanasian creed:

> For there is one person of the Father, another of the Son, and another of the Holy Spirit. But the Godhead of the Father, of the Son, and of the Holy Spirit is all one, the glory equal, the majesty coeternal. Such as the Father is, such is the Son, and such is the Holy Spirit. The Father uncreated, the Son uncreated, and the Holy Spirit uncreated. The Father incomprehensible, the Son incomprehensible, and the Holy Spirit incomprehensible. The Father eternal, the Son eternal, and the Holy Spirit eternal. And yet they are not three eternals but one eternal.[15]

## The Work of the Holy Spirit

The Holy Spirit is an active divine person. What is His work? Wayne Grudem writes, "The work of the Holy Spirit is to manifest the active presence of God in the world and especially in the church."[16] On the one hand, His work has always been to be "the power of God at work."[17] On the other hand, His work has had distinct eras.[18] The Holy Spirit's work in the era of "types" was to

---

14. Pink has a helpful section on the titles of the Holy Spirit that assist in proving His deity, *Holy Spirit*, 19–22.
15. Brannan, *Historic Creeds and Confessions*.
16. Grudem, *Systematic Theology*, 634.
17. Letham, *Holy Trinity*, 2019, 18.
18. Here I will consider the eras before and after Christ's appearance. The Spirit's work during the life, death and resurrection of Christ is in, e.g., Letham, *Holy Trinity*, 51–53; Pink, *Holy Spirit*, 31–37; and Berkhof, *Systematic Theology*, 98.

## The Practice of "Greater Works"

prepare God's people to receive her Messiah.[19] A brief list of these works include His work:

- Creating (Gen 1:2; Job 26:13; Ps 33:6, 104:30)
- Revealing God's truth (Num 24:2; 2 Sam 23:2; Job 32:8; Zech 7:12)
- Teaching God's people (Neh 9:20; Ps 143:10; Isa 48:16)
- Equipping people for leadership (Gen 41:38; Num 11:17; Deut 34:9; Judg 3:10, 6:34).[20]

The New Testament shines light on the Spirit's work in the Old, adding that He:

- Was Israel's guide (Acts 7:51)
- Brought the message of salvation to them (1 Pet 3:18)
- Authored the ritual worship (Heb 9:8)
- Spoke through David and the prophets (Matt 22:43; Mark 12:36; Acts 1:16, 28:25; 2 Pet 1:21) even predicting the Messiah's ministry (Luke 4:18–19).

B. B. Warfield summarizes this data by saying, "There can be no doubt that the New Testament writers identify the Holy Spirit of the New Testament with the Spirit of God of the Old."[21]

The Holy Spirit's work in the era of ectypes (that is, after the completed work of Christ), is no longer preparation for the Messiah but, according to J. I. Packer is, "to mediate the presence of our Lord Jesus Christ."[22] Warfield notes how we should think about the testamental differences in the work of the Holy Spirit:

19. Letham, *Holy Trinity*, 19.

20. The Old Testament record doesn't contain explicit word it was the Holy Spirit who endued the types of Christ (e.g., Moses, Melchizedek, or David) for their work. Yet if Robert Letham is correct and the Spirit is God's "power at work" then it is reasonable to assume the Spirit gifted them for their work. There is record He gifted some in the Old Testament for specific tasks (e.g., Bezalel, Exod 31:3–5).

21. Warfield, *Person and Work of the Holy Spirit*, 114.

22. Packer, *Keep in Step with the Spirit*, 49.

## Part Three | The Paradigm in Action

> The old dispensation was a preparatory one and must be strictly conceived as such.... The Spirit worked in providence no less universally then than now. He abode in the church not less really then than now. He wrought in the heart of God's people not less prevalently then than now. ... But the object of the whole dispensation was only to prepare for the outpouring of the Spirit upon all flesh.... The dispensation of the Spirit, properly so-called, did not dawn, however, until the period of preparation was over and the day of outpouring had come.[23]

Pink unpacks the Holy Spirit's work in this era in four heads. First, the Holy Spirit is to witness the exaltation of Christ, that is, in regenerating the elect, He makes the humiliation and exaltation of Christ known. Second, as we saw above, He is come to take Christ's place as the Guide and Comfort to His people. We saw in several places in John's gospel, the Lord declared both His departure and His Spirit's arrival as "another" Helper in His place. Third, "to further Christ's cause" that is "to interpret and vindicate Christ, to administer Christ in His Church and kingdom." And lastly, to endue Christ's servants, that is, to equip them for the works of ministry.[24]

Additionally, in a way consistent with this project, John Owen defines the Spirit's work as bringing to completion what the Father had planned to do through His Son.[25] The work of the Holy Spirit, here very briefly considered, sets the conditions for our consideration of the doctrine of spiritual gifts.

---

23. Warfield, *Person and Work of the Holy Spirit*, 118.

24. Pink, *Work of the Holy Spirit*, 46–47. Abraham Kuyper wrote, "We have seen the work of the Holy Spirit consists in leading all creation to its destiny, the final purpose of which is the glory of God." Kuyper, *Work of the Holy Spirit*, 23.

25. Owen, *The Holy Spirit*, 21. In Winslow's framework, that work is to (a) quicken, (b) indwell, (c) sanctify and (d) seal believers, Winslow, *Work of the Holy Spirit*, 9.

*The Practice of "Greater Works"*

## SECTION 2: THE DOCTRINE OF SPIRITUAL GIFTS

As we noted in our study of John 14:12–14, Jesus promised the church would do His works and greater works still. Connecting this passage together with Eph 4:7–12, we may deduce these manifestations of the Spirit are specifically for the purpose of doing the greater works Jesus promised.[26] Therefore, these individual manifestations of the Spirit are gifts in the areas of the prophetic, the priestly, and the kingly.[27]

Spiritual gifts (or roles) are an essential component of the life and work of the local church; it is now how the greater works of Christ get done. The apostle Paul writes in 1 Cor 12:4–7,

> Now there are varieties of gifts, but the same Spirit; and there are varieties of service, but the same Lord; and there are varieties of activities, but it is the same God who empowers them all in everyone. To each is given the manifestation of the Spirit for the common good.

In this central passage, we are taught each believer is endued with a manifestation of the Spirit, variously called "gifts," "service," and "activities." The exercise of these gifts classified as prophetic, priestly, and kingly is governed by ten principles derived from Scripture.

## Ten Guiding Principles of Spiritual Gifts

First, the work of Christ through gifts is God's sovereign work: He gives to whom He wills (1 Cor 12:11, 18), "All these [gifts] are empowered by one and the same Spirit, who apportions to each one individually as He wills. . . . But as it is, God arranged the members

---

26. Indeed, the context of John 14:15–17 connected Jesus' promise of greater works with the provision of greater work, that is, the provision of the Holy Spirit.

27. Gladd, *From Adam and Israel to the Church*, 116. Vern Poythress makes this point clearly, "All the gifts mentioned in Romans 12, 1 Corinthians 12 and Ephesians 4 can be roughly classified as prophetic, kingly or priestly." Poythress, "Modern Spiritual Gifts as Analogous to Apostolic Gifts," 72.

in the body, each one of them, as He chose." Any discussion of spiritual gifts must begin with the sovereign distribution of God.

Secondly, the gifts are good. In 1 Cor 12:4 Paul wrote, "Now there are varieties of gifts, but the same Spirit; and there are varieties of service, but the same Lord." First Peter 4:10 affirms, "As each has received a gift, use it to serve one another, as good stewards of God's varied grace."[28] These verses indicate that gifts are graces that "w[ere] given" (Eph 4:7, cf. 1 Cor 12:7a).

These opportunities for serving the Lord and the church are meant to bring joy and blessings to the church. Of course, spiritual gifts contain the burden of use as God's expectation is we use the gifts He's given us for His glory and the good of the church. Still, inherent in the burden is the beauty of the gift; they are good since they come down from the Father of lights (Jas 1:17).

Further, in 1 Cor 12:4–7, Paul uses five Greek words to unpack the English word "gift," and in their definitions we can see their gracious nature. Paul opens the discussion about the gifts as manifestations of the Holy Spirit, things that are "spiritual [things] (12:1)."[29] This comes from the base Greek word for "Spirit" (*pneuma*). Of course it is correct to see these manifestations of the Spirit as equipment for ministry yet we cannot neglect to recognize each believer has a glorious endowment of God within (e.g., 2 Tim 1:14; Jas 4:5).

Paul also tells us that these come to us graciously: they are *charisma*: (12:4)[30] from the verb "to give graciously." They aren't for personal advancement but corporate benefit through service. This is obvious as they are also called *diakonia* (12:5) a "service" or "ministry."[31] We are not left to our own power or strength to do this work as they are also called *energma* (12:6) the "activities" or workings of the power of the Spirit. They are, after all *phanerosis*, (12:7) that is, "manifestations" of the Holy Spirit.[32] H. Parks wrote,

28. See also Rom 12:3.
29. *BAGD*, 679.
30. *BAGD*, 878.
31. *BAGD*, 184.
32. *BAGD*, 853.

## The Practice of "Greater Works"

Here is grace taking substance, grace becoming concrete and tangible. There are some who prefer grace without gifts. To insist that grace be without gifts is to frustrate the very grace of God. Gifts exist in order that grace may come out of the abstract into the concrete, that grace may have some[thing] to offer. If faith without works is dead, so likewise grace without gifts.[33]

The third biblical principle about spiritual gifts is that each gift is powered by the Holy Spirit (1 Cor 12:4–6). They aren't simply manifestations of the Spirit (12:7); they are kingdom tools empowered by the Spirit. Using Packer's definition, spiritual gifts are "Actualized powers of expressing, celebrating, displaying and so communicating Christ in one way or another, either by word or deed."[34] This definition is important for it keeps us anchored in what the Spirit is actually doing in the world, that is, finishing the work of Christ by giving gifts to us and working through us.

Gifts in the local church are given by the Spirit and empowered by the Spirit. This is the clear conclusion of Christ's sending "another Helper." That is, God is the active party working in and through the gifts.[35] Zechariah 4:6 is a good summary of what this means, "Then he said to me, "This is the word of the LORD to Zerubbabel: Not by might, nor by power, but by my Spirit, says the LORD of hosts."

Fourth, each believer has a gift that he gets at conversion (1 Cor 12:7; cf. Eph 4:7, Rom 12:3), "To each is given the manifestation of the Spirit for the common good." David Garland writes, "But the metaphor of the bodily members (12:12–26) suggests Paul believes that each member (cf. 3:5, 13; 7:17) in the church has been given a gift and function."[36] Textual clues that Paul is talking about each individual member is also found in his regular use of

---

33. Cited in Elbert, "Calvin and the Spiritual Gifts," 238.

34. Packer, *Keep in Step with the Spirit*, 83. They are "Abilities that God has granted to Christians for the edification of others in the body and the evangelization of those outside the body," Mack and Swavely, *Life in the Father's House*, 146.

35. Riddlebarger, *First Corinthians*, 320.

36. Fee, *God's Empowering Presence*, 163. Garland, *1 Corinthians*, 577.

the singular dative in the verses that follow. In support of this view, each gift has a dual purpose, first, as the means of doing the greater works of Christ and second, as a manifestation "of the Spirit," that is, an objective evidence of saving faith in the individual.[37]

Fifth, each believer's gift is unique to him and equal to all others at the same time. Paul makes this clear in 1 Cor 12:12, 14–31: "For just as the body is one and has many members, and all the members of the body, though many, are one body, so it is with Christ." Consider the principles from 12:14–31 that locate each individual believer's giftedness in the context of the broader church:

a. 12:14: one body, many members

b. 12:15–16: all belong and none can despise the other

c. 12:17–18: all are needed for balance and effectiveness

d. 12:18: each is placed there by God's design

e. 12:22: all are essential no matter their function

f. 12:25: we have to care for each other, gifts notwithstanding

g. 12:27: we are each ("individually") members of each other

h. 12:28: God has appointed roles and gifts

Sixth, the gifts are specifically endowments of the Holy Spirit; they are manifestations of His presence and activity. This principle explains the gifts are given by the Spirit, empowered by the Spirit and for use in the Spirit's pursuit of the work of Christ. Before one was converted, he had no such manifestation (cf. 1 Cor 2:14). The full implications of this are not clear. In other words, there is not a uniform answer to this question: "With the coming of the Spirit, does He 'convert' natural abilities into spiritual gifts or does He give something brand new?" Wayne Grudem thinks the former is true: "A spiritual gift is any ability that is empowered by the Holy Spirit and used in any ministry of the church."[38] Packer seems to agree,

---

37. I take that genitive as subjective.

38 Grudem, *Systematic Theology*, 1016. C. Peter Wagner disagrees: "Spiritual gifts are not to be regarded as dedicated natural talents." Wagner, *Your Spiritual Gifts Can Help Your Church Grow*, 77.

stating, "the most significant gifts in the church's life (preaching, teaching, leadership, counsel, support) are ordinarily natural abilities sanctified."[39]

A practical caution, however, is our very human tendency to maximize some roles and gifts and minimize others perhaps due in part to believing that the gifts are simply extensions of natural talents. But God grants roles and abilities to Christians for the edification of the body and the evangelization of those outside the body. It seems clear that men and women were simply not caught up in the redemptive purposes of God for His glory until they were converted. This makes the gifts the tools in God's hands to bring about spiritual maturity, that is salvation and growth in Christ's likeness.

Of the view shared by Grudem and Packer, Kim Riddlebarger is more cautious:

> While these gifts may be related to the natural abilities people already have (in the sense that spiritual gifts are a supernatural enhancement of our natural abilities), Paul's comments throughout this section [1 Cor 12] emphasize the fact that the charismata are divine endowments given specifically for the building up of the church and the edification of its members.[40]

Indeed, we may be closer to an answer by classifying the spiritual gifts as we are in this project, namely as prophetic, priestly, or kingly. These were exercised severally in the Old Testament through types not within the broader cultural context but among the people of God and in Israel, respectively. They were fulfilled in Christ's work as our mediator and distributed to the church for the completion of greater end-time works.

---

39. Packer, *Keep in Step with the Spirit*, 29. He gives the following caveat: "We need to draw a clear distinction between man's capacity to perform and God's prerogative to bless, for it is God's use of our abilities rather than the abilities themselves that constitute charismata. If no regular, identifiable spiritual benefit for others or ourselves results from what we do, we should not think of our capacity to do it as a spiritual gift," 71.

40. Riddlebarger, *1 Corinthians*, 318.

## Part Three | The Paradigm in Action

Although, if the gift lists are representative and not exhaustive (see below), we cannot outright limit what constitutes a gift. But that is not to say we are not helped in understanding what they are for and where God intends them to be used. Perhaps the most we can say is to agree with Riddlebarger: a spiritual gift is an endowment of the Holy Spirit given to each believer for the good of the church.[41] Whether that endowment was something novel[42] or something present that was redeemed and deployed by the Spirit, its results (see below) will indicate whether it could be called a "spiritual gift."

The seventh principle concerning spiritual gifts is that they are for the edification of and service to the church. John Calvin said, "Whatever benefits we obtain from the Lord have been entrusted to us on this condition: that they be applied to the common good of the church."[43] Additionally, the apostle Paul is very specific on the purpose of the gifts. They are for the "common good" (*sumphero*; lit. "carry together;" 1 Cor 12:7),[44] for the "building up of the body of Christ" (Eph 4:11–14).

As with the vexing question about the nature of spiritual gifts, that is, whether they are new gifts or repurposed abilities, we may not be able to determine if the Spirit's gifts are intended for use outside the church as well as inside.[45] The context of passages

---

41. When believers find themselves excelling in what appears to be prophet, priest, or king roles outside the local church, it could be for one or more of three reasons. Prophetic: excellence in communication is a doorway by which God intends to draw people into His kingdom by His word. Priestly: excellence in helping people walk through life is a doorway by which God seeks to welcome people to join Him in life. Kingly: excellence at order making is a doorway by which God intends to demonstrate His order and rule. Perhaps we could call these "outward looking" faces. In all the spheres outside the assembled local church, God's people are His ambassadors displaying His glory and He may use spiritual gifts to do this.

42. In some cases it surely was such as speaking in unknown tongues, words of knowledge or wisdom or healings.

43. Elbert, "Calvin and Spiritual Gifts," 238.

44. Thomas, *New American Standard Hebrew-Aramaic and Greek Dictionaries : Updated Edition*.

45. The latter seems more likely to me. Richard Belcher seems to support

## The Practice of "Greater Works"

like Rom 12 ("measure of faith that God has assigned" 12:3), 1 Cor 11–14 (corporate church life), Eph 4 (cited above) and 1 Pet 4 ("that in everything God may be glorified through Jesus Christ," 4:11) seems to argue for the use of spiritual gifts in the church alone. Packer states, "We are told that gifts, rightly used, build up Christians and churches."[46]

Eighth, related to the third principle above, is the centrality of accountability in the practice of spiritual gifts. First, the believer is accountable to the Lord for his apprehension and use of the manifestation of the Spirit. In this way, prayer in the proper use of a spiritual gift is essential. For example, a new convert must pray that the Spirit would give him opportunities to serve in the local church, clarifying His gifting. When the use of a gift seems to bring some pressure on the church, the believer must include prayer to the Lord to reveal if the practice of the gift is poorly done or if the motive behind its practice is ungodly. Secondly, the believer in the local body is accountable to the elders of that body. The elders, held responsible by the Lord for the spiritual condition of the local flock, must have the freedom to weigh in a believer's use of a gift. This is especially true when the use of the gift is causing discord, division, or pressure on the church.

The ninth principle regards the nature of the gift lists. I believe they are illustrative of the kinds of work to be done rather than exhaustive lists of the only ways in which the work can be done. There are several lines of proof for this. First, while the Spirit reveals lists of gifts (Rom 12:3–8[47]; 1 Cor 12:8–10, 28; Eph 4:11 and 1 Pet 4:10–11), it is unclear that the texts themselves should lead

---

them operating in both, Belcher, *Prophet, Priest, and King*, 179–80.

46. Packer, *Concise Theology: A Guide to Historic Christian Beliefs*, 227. However, it might be true if, for example, one is kingly gifted that he is able to give order or oversee chaotic or disorganized bodies outside as well as inside the church.

47. Compare Rom 12:9: "let love be genuine" seems to imply what went before would unpack "love" as well as suggest that all the enumerated gifts weren't meant to be comprehensive but illustrative of how to love the brethren. Is Rom 12:13 a "gift" of mercy? If so, why isn't it listed?

us to conclude they are exhaustive.[48] Paul wrote each letter to these churches for specific reasons including gifts pertinent to their experience or that needed his specific guidance.[49] Second, there is overlap in the common sense understanding of some of the gifts: e.g., administration (1 Cor 12:28) and leadership (Rom 12:8); prophecy (Eph 4:11) and speaking for God (1 Pet 4:11). Third, in some cases an activity is listed (prophecy: Rom 12:6) while in others a person or role is listed (prophet: Eph 4:11). Fourth, the lists also contain gifts that are tantamount to categories: "serving" (Rom 12:6) or "helps" (1 Cor 12:28). Lastly, no Bible book listing gifts contains the same list. It is for reasons like these that Grudem concludes, "These facts indicate that Paul was not attempting to construct exhaustive lists of gifts when he specified the ones he did. Although there is sometimes an indication of some order . . . it seems that in general Paul was almost randomly listing a series of different examples of gifts as they came to mind.[50] I concur.

The last principle is that the proper use of gifts will have certain results. If we cannot conclude whether a spiritual gift is a novel endowment or a redeemed existing talent, the results of the proper use of the manifestation of the Spirit are also criteria for whether the exercise of an activity or service is a spiritual gift. The questions to ask for verification should include:

> Does the gift bring honor to Christ (1 Cor 12:1–3) or does it throw glory on the one using it?

As we have seen in our study, the Father and the Son sent the Holy Spirit to apply the work of Christ to the elect. This application was indeed the substitutionary atonement of the Lord Jesus Christ but also the enduements necessary to do the greater works Jesus promised to the church. If one claims to have a manifestation of the Spirit, then his claim would be supported by both the display

---

48. Hodge, *First and Second Corinthians*, 244; Ciampa and Rosner, *First Letter to the Corinthians*, 572.

49. We could assert the same is happening in the letters to the seven churches in Rev 1–3.

50. Grudem, *Systematic Theology*, 1020.

## The Practice of "Greater Works"

of the fruit of the Spirit (showing the application of the atonement) as well as the gifts of the Spirit (showing participation in the remaining work of Christ).

> Does the exercise of the gift serve to mature the whole body or does its use cause division (1 Cor 12:4–11; Eph 4:13–15)?

Clearly a purpose of the gifts of the Spirit is the building up of the body of Christ. This building up might include stern teaching or preaching for the restoration of holiness or mission and that would pressure the church to repentance. However, that is different than the use of a gift producing consistent discord or confusion. For example, in Paul's first letter to the Corinthians, his aim was clearly to correct their practices as they were not building up the church but halting its growth and disturbing its unity.

> Does the exercise of the gift make the ministry of the church more effective in kingdom expansion (Eph 4:15–16)?

Related to the previous question, this one evaluates the effectiveness of the church in its ministry. In many contexts, the faithful and efficient use of the gifts of the Spirit should lead to increased attendance at worship, larger volunteer base, more conversions, more baptisms or more churches planted. In other contexts, those gripped by persecution, these metrics may be present but it is more likely effectiveness is measured in the depth of the display of the fruits of the Spirit.

> Does the use of the gift foster unity and love for each other or envy and discord (1 Cor 12:12–13, 27–31; Eph 4:13)?

It is tempting to measure effective use of the gifts of the Spirit in the tangible metrics listed above. However, criteria must also include evidence of stronger covenant community. The consistent testimony of the Scripture is to kingdom expansion resulting from covenant community (cf. Acts 2:44–47; John 17:20–23), that is, greater love and unity among the church. Believers in a local church should welcome the powerful display of the gifts of the

Spirit done properly, that is, in love. Knowing it is through means such as these the Lord is growing His church and beating back the gates of hell.

> Does the use of the gift bring honor and help to others (12:14–20)?

An obvious criteria for whether one has a manifestation of the Spirit is if it brings honor and help to others in the body. Heidelberg Catechism question 55 highlights this: "What do you understand by the 'communion of the saints'?"

> First, that all and every one who believes, being members of Christ, as in common, partakers of Him and of all His riches and gifts; secondly, that every one must know it to be his duty, readily and cheerfully to employ his gifts, for the advantage and salvation of other members.[51]

Paul insisted that the church use the gifts the Lord has given (Rom 12:6). Further in Rom 12, after the exhortation to use the gifts, he urges the church to a manner of covenant life characterized by mutual help and love: "If possible, so far as it depends on you, live peaceably with all" (12:18). It seems clear the use of spiritual gifts is for the purpose of meeting this challenge.

## SECTION 3: THE PRACTICE OF GREATER WORKS: THE GIFT LISTS AND THE OFFICES

The gift lists in the New Testament are ready examples of the ways in which the church does the greater works of Christ. As noted above, the challenge in our day is in understanding how to approach the gift lists as well as how to use them to assist us in finding our place in the local church to serve. The thesis of this project is the superior usefulness of the PPK paradigm for this effort.

In the last chapter, we will present a model for local church ministry based on this paradigm. In preparation for using this

---

51. Beeke and Ferguson, *Reformed Confessions Harmonized*, Annotated Edition, 198.

## The Practice of "Greater Works"

paradigm, in this final section we will introduce working definitions for the ministry of the ectypes in the church as well as survey the lists of gifts found in the New Testament and coordinate them according to the three offices of prophet, priest, and king.

### Working Definitions for Ectype Ministry

Prophets of the greater works "convey the will of God" in accord with the Scriptures. This conveyance captures the prophet's role from of old, through the ministry of the Lord Jesus and into the church age. In the Old Testament as well as the early church, the prophet was usually prevailed upon by the Lord and given a message to convey immediately (that is, from God directly). In this age, with the end of the founding era of the church, prophets no longer receive direct revelation from the Lord but pass on what has been written down in God's word.[52]

Priests of the greater works "assist in the application of the conveyed will of God." Priests are partners with the prophets in assisting the church in growing like Christ through prayer, counsel, and teaching. Once again, this duty was seen in the priests of old: the covenant prosecutors, the prophets, required priest-action on behalf of the people. The cultic duties of the old covenant priests was fulfilled in the once-for-all sacrifice of Christ, yet in Christ and in the church, intercession, advocacy, service, and counsel remain priestly duties.

Kings of the greater works "restore or order the church." Again, in partnership with the prophets and priests, the king makes it possible for the former to do their greater work. A king's concerns is to create and maintain the necessary order so the building and growing of the church is unhindered.

---

52. In Pentecostal traditions, it is believed prophets still receive direct revelation from God. In my judgment, if that view is held, what is received from the Lord would be wholly consistent with His revealed and written word.

Part Three | The Paradigm in Action

## Correlating NT Gifts with the "Prophet, Priest, King" paradigm

If the PPK is a biblical paradigm, it will accommodate the biblical data. In other words, we should not have to "shoehorn" the biblical data into the model but rather see it fall in place appropriately. In Figure 1 below, I have used the definitions for the prophets, priests, and kings and have correlated the listed gifts accordingly.

As we can see from Figure 1, if the hard work of investigating whether a believer is gifted as a prophet, priest, or king is completed, then the next step is to determine what in the church can be done.[53] The listed gifts can further lead a person to invest himself in that ministry of the local church. At the same time, local church ministry might be more or less specific than the gifts listed. Having confirmed whether one is primarily gifted as a prophet, priest, or king will provide a ready way to overcome this issue.

---

53. This step is also subject to other biblical constraints. For example, a woman gifted as a prophet or a king would also have to abide by 1 Tim 2:12: "I do not permit a woman to teach or to exercise authority over a man; rather, she is to remain quiet."

## The Practice of "Greater Works"

| | Prophetic: conveying | Priestly: assisting | Kingly: ordering |
|---|---|---|---|
| | **1 Corinthians 12:4–11** | | |
| 12:8 | the utterance of wisdom[54] | | |
| | the utterance of knowledge | | |
| 12:9 | | faith | |
| | | gifts of healing | |
| 12:10 | prophecy | the working of miracles | |
| | various kinds of tongues | | the ability to distinguish between spirits |
| | the interpretation of tongues | | |
| 12:28 | prophets | miracles | apostles |
| | teachers | gifts of healing | administrating |
| | various kinds of tongues | helping | |
| | **Romans 12:3–8** | | |
| 12:6b | if prophecy | | |
| 12:7 | the one who teaches | if service, in our serving | |
| 12:8 | the one who exhorts | the one who contributes | the one who leads |
| | | the one who does acts of mercy | |
| | **1 Peter 4:7–11** | | |
| 4:11 | whoever speaks | | |
| | | whoever serves | |
| | **Ephesians 4:11** | | |
| 4:11 | the prophets | the shepherds | the apostles |
| | the teachers | | the evangelists |

**Figure 1.**

---

54. As with all the gifts historically called the "miraculous" gifts (like the "utterance of wisdom," or "various kinds of tongues") whether such a gift persists in the modern era cannot be decided using the PPK. Instead, broader redemptive-historical or systematic-theological principles must come into play. Whether "cessationist" or "continuationalist," however, the paradigm is largely unaffected.

# CHAPTER SIX

## The PPK Model for Local Church Ministry

IN PARTS TWO AND three, we considered the biblical basis for the Prophet, Priest, and King paradigm for use in the local church. In this final chapter, we gather up that biblical data for the purpose of more strictly defining the office-roles. That way, once the PPKa is completed, a congregant can press forward in serving the church.

### SIMPLE DEFINITIONS

Prophet. The prophet "conveys the will of God."

Above we noted this was an implicit duty given to Adam, namely, that he would pass on to Eve and their children the instructions given to him by the Lord. As we have already seen in our study, the prophetic role sometimes involved receiving a direct revelation from God and sometimes passing on the received revelation of God. In both cases, the prophet's responsibility was to convey the will of God to the people. Prophets of the former order have passed from the church with the giving of the written word of God. Prophets of the latter order convey (that is, teach, preach, or counsel) the written word of God; this constitutes the burden of those gifted to do the greater prophetic works.[1]

## Priest. The priest "assists in the application of the revealed will of God."

This also was a task originally given to Adam in the garden of Eden. He was told to keep and cultivate for the benefit of his family, that is facilitate the true worship of God and interpersonal love in his family.[2] Priests are still advocates for "their" people with the Lord and for one another. Priests of old offered gifts, sacrifices, and prayer. The Lord Jesus was the archetype in this way, giving Himself as gift and sacrifice and praying for the church in both His humiliation (e.g., John 17:9, Heb 5:7) and exaltation (Heb 7:25). With the once-for-all sacrifice of Christ, the priests' responsibilities to preside over gifts and oblations has passed away. The ministry of intercession remains yet that was never their only responsibility; they were teachers who would assist in applying the revealed word of God to the people (e.g., Lev 10:11; Neh 8:2, 8).[3] The burden of those gifted to do the greater priestly works now engage in assisting (through, e.g., counseling-teaching and prayer) the church.

## King. The king "restores or orders the church."

Part of man's created role is to rule as vice-regent for the Lord (Gen 9:1–7, cf. Gen 1:28). Berkhof, referring to the king, asserts kings restore broken creation.[4] By definition that requires making order out of chaos. Kings made order in the development and

---

1. "Greater prophetic works" combines the "greater works" of John 14 with the prophetic office of the paradigm.

2. These were terms later applied to the Old Testament priests.

3. This point was well made in Timothy Paul Jones: "Based on the priestly roles described throughout the Old Testament, it seems that the primary responsibility of priests in disputed legal cases may have been to teach and to apply precepts found in the Torah." "Prophets, Priests and Kings Today?," 73.

4. Berkhof, *Systematic Theology*, 357.

government of their kingdoms. It is clear in the church, roles like these fall to elders and deacons (e.g., 1 Tim 3:4, 12). Yet hints that this belongs to the broader church are found in places like Matt 18 and in named gifts like "administration" (1 Cor 12:28). This is the burden of those who are gifted to do the greater kingly works.

## EXPANDED DEFINITIONS

Unlike the Lord Jesus, the roles of prophet, priest, and king are not all found in one person; they are distributed to the body of Christ (cf. 1 Cor 12:11; Eph 4:8). In Figure 1, this distribution is depicted along the three lines of the paradigm.

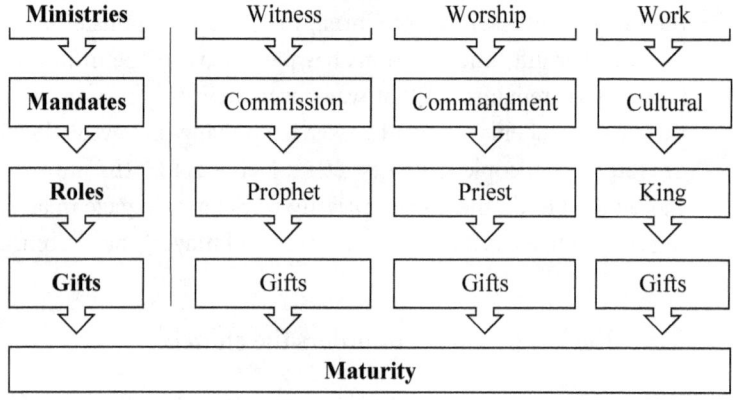

**Figure 1.**

The ministry of "witness," founded upon Adam's responsibility to convey the will of God to his family, was given to the church in the words of the Great Commission (Matt 28:18–20). Our general prophetic mission is to evangelize, baptize, and teach the church.

The ministry of "worship," the highest application of the conveyed word of God, also given to Adam, was given to the church in the two great commandments (Matt 22:37–39). Our general

## The PPK Model for Local Church Ministry

priestly mission is to apply God's word in the areas of worship and service.

Lastly, the ministry of "work" finds its root in the original charge to Adam (Gen 1:28) and its renewal with Noah (Gen 9:1, 7) that endures to this day.

The church, then, has prophetic, priestly, and kingly missions. It should also be evident that the Spirit distributes these responsibilities according to His sovereign will, giving, as Paul teaches in his letters, different endowments of the Spirit to different believers. Consider Figure 2 which combines these concepts together:

**Priest**
**Great Commandments**
**Worship**

Figure 2.

Figure 2 depicts a way to understand the various gifting of the Holy Spirit in the local church: a Spirit overseen congregation of prophets, priests, and kings. At the center, the perfect prophet, priest, and king is the Lord Jesus. Since He has given the church the task to do His works and greater still, by His Spirit He distributes the offices to the church as He sees fit and as they have need.

## Part Three | The Paradigm in Action

The triangle contains all the work of the local church while making room for its members to be differently gifted. In order to assess how the Spirit has gifted each church member, he or she will submit to the Prophet-Priest-King Assessment (PPKa). We will discuss this tool below, but first, using Figure 2 above, we will suggest expanded definitions of these roles.

As we will see in the PPKa, for test-takers many times, scores between the top two areas can be close. This is expected since the types of the Old Testament had overlapping tasks even if they had one that was primary.[5] Indeed, in the church some would have great passion for teaching the Word (prophet) but also dearly love to pray for people in need (priest). We could call them "prophet-priests" or "priest-prophets" depending on the scores of their assessment. The following expanded definitions assist local church members in interpreting their scores.

*Keywords.*[6]

a. Prophet: revelation
b. Priest: application
c. King: organization

*Expanded definitions.*

Top Score: **Prophet**. The prophet conveys the will of God as contained in the Scriptures. A prophet is God's "mouthpiece," that is he or she is God's advocate of His word. Some are set apart and ordained for the task (e.g., pastors, teaching or ruling elders). Others whose top score is "prophet" are committed to convey God's word to people in exhortation, correction, defense, or evangelism.

---

5. For example, priests who offered sacrifices and taught the law and kings who built temples and offered prayer for the nation.
6. The "keywords" further help the church member to sort his own scores.

## The PPK Model for Local Church Ministry

Prophet-king. REVELATION + ORGANIZATION[7]

a. Purpose: Prophet-kings are committed to convey God's word in an ordered, stable environment.

b. Ministry: For this person, being a Word-conveyer is primary (i.e., "prophet" is the top score), that is teaching, preaching, witnessing, apologetics as highest commitments. The kingly side encourages developing, ordering, or reforming ministries *for* the organized and effective proclamation of the word.

c. Examples of context. Teaching in an established organization large or small. If unavailable, developing the organization so teaching can be done.

d. Possible biblical examples: Deborah[8] (Judg 4:4–9), Samuel (1 Sam 7:3, 5–11), Ezra (Ezra 8:15–36), Paul (Acts 14:19–23), Timothy (1 Tim 4:6–16).

e. Local church examples: Church planter, church revitalization, group teacher (e.g., Sunday school, Bible study, or conference), ministry developer (creating, leading, or reforming), ministry consultant (evaluate, discern, or direct) or curriculum writer.

Prophet-priest. REVELATION + APPLICATION

a. Purpose: To convey the word in order to make a direct impact on someone's life.

b. Ministry: For this person, being a Word-conveyer is primary: teaching, witnessing, and defending are the highest commitments. The priestly side seeks to have a "front-row seat" to the application of the Word; seeks to train another in wise decision-making.

---

7. In combining these keywords, we see both the possible priority and connectedness between them.

8. The OT examples, though "types" and not "ectypes" strictly speaking, demonstrated some of the gifting under the different office categories.

Part Three | The Paradigm in Action

    c. Examples of context: The audience is smaller, i.e., one-on-one or in a small group. This person is an accountability partner, coach or a mentor to others.

    d. Possible biblical examples: Elijah (1 Kgs 17:8–16, 18:18–19), John the Baptist (Matt 3:1–12), Peter (Acts 10), Philip (Acts 8:26–39), Priscilla (Acts 18:26).

    e. Local church examples: evangelism or apologetics, "Titus 2" mentor, street preacher, biblical counseling, praying, small group teaching or leading.

Top Score: **Priest**. The priest assists in the application of the revealed will of God. He is God's representative helping to apply the blessings of our salvation to others. He encourages and facilitates direct access to God. Priests plead that God would bend His power on behalf of the people. Priests lead the people in enjoying that power. Priests are agents of God's compassion, mercy, help and giving.

    Priest-prophet. APPLICATION + REVELATION

    a. Purpose: To assist people in living godly and wise lives being conformed to Christ.

    b. Ministry: For this person, partnership in applying the Word is primary. A Word-centered servant looking for creative ways to help people apply the word. This person is a mentor committed to biblical truth-telling.

    c. Examples of context: These people accept others with an agenda to grow in Christ. These are servants who are helping, serving, and assisting.

    d. Possible biblical examples: Abigail (1 Sam 25:23–31), the apostle John (3 John), Barnabas (Acts 9:27), Aquila (Acts 18:26), Epaphroditus (Phil 2:25–29), "Titus 2 woman."

    e. Local church examples: prayer partner, biblical counseling, liturgist, music ministry, diaconal ministry, small group teaching, fellowship or community planner.

## The PPK Model for Local Church Ministry

Priest-king. APPLICATION + ORGANIZATION

a. Purpose: To ensure the organization effectively facilitates wise living: to serve the people with an ordered and effective organization.

b. Ministry: Applying the Word is very important to this person. Organization, more than teaching, however, is a key to the success of this.

c. Examples of context: Having a helpful and efficient organization (no matter the size) is key. However, this person believes flexibility and intimacy should be the senior partners over order and structure.

d. Possible biblical examples: Zerubbabel, James (Acts 15:13–21)

e. Local church examples: Ministry team leader, clerk of a governing body, diaconal ministry (ordained and non-ordained), sound/AV tech, nursery organizer, welcome-assimilation, ministry department chairs, "behind the scenes" person.

Top Score: **King**. The king orders the ministry organization. The church's work must be led, managed, changed, protected and guided. There are times when its government is set apart, ordained and installed and other times in other parts of the work when it is not necessary to be so.

King-prophet. ORGANIZATION + REVELATION

a. Purpose: To organize and structure to facilitate ministry of the Word: to serve the revealing of God's word.

b. Ministry: Revitalizes, reorders, develops opportunities for conveying the Word; teaches, orders, and governs by biblical precept and principle (e.g., church officers and discipline, regulative principle of worship).

c. Examples of context: The organization is a key means to help advance truth. Processes are very important part of the structure but only if they serve preaching or teaching the word. Target the long term benefit to overcome short term pain.

Part Three | The Paradigm in Action

    d. Possible biblical examples: Moses, Paul (Acts 20:7–12), Barnabas (Acts 9:26–27, 15:39–40), John (1 John 2:1–6).

    e. Local church examples: organizing pastor, church planter, "ruling" elder, new ministry developer, ministry reformer, curriculum writer.

    King-priest. ORGANIZATION + APPLICATION

    a. Purpose: To make the organization helpful in promoting wise living: to serve the people in the ministry through the organization.

    b. Ministry: An administrator or implementer. Helping (or applying) is very important, and policies and order are the pathways to accomplish this.

    c. Examples of context: Large or small, structured for effective help. This person sees the organization as an essential means to help people. This person believes order and structure should be the senior partners over flexibility and intimacy.

    d. Possible biblical examples: Jethro (Exod 18:10–23), Joseph (Gen 41:37–49), Naomi (Ruth 2:19–23), Peter (1 Pet 5:1–11).

    e. Examples: administrators, HR staff, deacons, ruling elders, ministry secretaries or chairmen and diaconate chairmen.

In Figure 3, there is a combination of this data. The design with this chart is to further assist church members as they consider their assessment results.

## The PPK Model for Local Church Ministry

| Witness<br>Commission<br>Prophet | Worship<br>Commandments<br>Priest | Work<br>Cultural Mandate<br>King |
|---|---|---|
| Teach | Listening | Director |
| Preach | Prayer | Staff leader |
| Correct | Interceding | Build |
| Discipline | Represent | Procedures |
| Rebuke | Music | Policy |
| Reproof | Counseling | Count |
| Witness | Mentoring | Systematize |
| Apologist | Giving | Plan |
| Write | Serving | Organize |
| Exhortation | Mercy acts | Leader |
| Discerning | Pastor / shepherd | Defend / protect |
| Witness | Compassion | Administrator |
| Evangelize | Mentors | Overseer |
| Coaching | Encouragement | Finance |
| | People | Visionary |
| | Mediating | Resourcing |
| | | Gather |
| | | Hospitality |
| | | Cooking |
| | | Tasks |

**Figure 3.**

## THE PROPHET-PRIEST-KING ASSESSMENT (PPKA)

The heart of this project is the PPKa. This assessment differs from other spiritual gift inventories in the following ways. First, it draws from a biblical ministry paradigm, the "Prophet, Priest, and King" paradigm. As we have seen, this is well-established in Scripture. Second, it is the result of weaving together Jesus' teaching in John

## Part Three | The Paradigm in Action

14 and the apostles' teaching in Eph 4 and other places (e.g., Rom 8, 1 Cor 12, 1 Pet 4). Third, it does not introduce extra-biblical criteria for evaluating the spiritual giftedness of a believer (e.g., psychology). Fourth, it is not dependent upon any particular family of theological understanding or doctrinal position.[9] Making distinctions in these ways does not depend on the PPKa but on the interpretation of other Scriptures or historic doctrinal commitments. Fifth, it includes external evaluation of assessment scores to provide an objective look at the scores. Sixth, its design targets a top score only (e.g., prophet or priest or king). The trailing scores clarify the ministry opportunities for the top score. For example, if a test-taker's top score is "king" and the next score is "priest," then the test-taker could seek a kingly role in the administration of a church's ministry e.g., the nursery.

For the PPKa to be effective four things are required. First, zeal to serve the Lord in the manner He has prescribed; a test-taker cannot simply think that doing whatever comes into his mind constitutes spiritual ministry. Secondly, pray before, during, and after answering the questions; he is seeking to determine the best place to use his spiritual gift and must seek the Spirit's guidance in the effort. Thirdly, commitment to historic biblical inerrancy, sufficiency, and authority.[10] The assessment depends on Scripture for its design, its questions,[11] and its implementation. Lastly, one must be part of a local church providing an objective analysis of a person's scores.

The assessment has three sections. Each section contains twenty questions that pertain to that office. Each question is scored using a five-point scale and evaluation notes of "Never" (scored at 1), "Seldom" (scored at 2), "On occasion" (scored at 3), "Often" (scored at 4), and "Regularly" (scored at 5). At the end, there is a

---

9. E.g., dispensationalism or covenant theology, cessationism or "continuationism," Calvinism or Arminianism.

10. For example, the *Westminster Confession of Faith*, chapter 1. See also Grudem, *Systematic Theology*, part 1.

11. Strictly speaking, the questions aren't quotes from the Bible but are drawn from aspects of each of the roles as they are defined and exemplified in the Bible.

short explanatory narrative and questions a mentor should ask the one who took the assessment to "test" the results.

## PROPHET.

1. Do you see people in need of corrected thinking, right understanding, or sound doctrine?

   | Never (1) | Seldom (2) | On occasion (3) | Often (4) | Regularly (5) |
   |---|---|---|---|---|
   |  |  |  |  |  |

2. Are you burdened to share the Word of God with others?

   | Never | Seldom | On occasion | Often | Regularly |
   |---|---|---|---|---|
   |  |  |  |  |  |

3. Would most of your close people call you a "truth-teller"?

   | Never | Seldom | On occasion | Often | Regularly |
   |---|---|---|---|---|
   |  |  |  |  |  |

4. Do you find yourself questioning non-biblical worldviews or belief systems?

   | Never | Seldom | On occasion | Often | Regularly |
   |---|---|---|---|---|
   |  |  |  |  |  |

5. Do you get into theological topics in conversations with people?

   | Never | Seldom | On occasion | Often | Regularly |
   |---|---|---|---|---|
   |  |  |  |  |  |

## Part Three | The Paradigm in Action

6. Read 1 Thess 5:14. Do you find yourself more interested in "admonishing the idle" than "encouraging the fainthearted"?

| Never | Seldom | On occasion | Often | Regularly |
|---|---|---|---|---|
|  |  |  |  |  |

7. Is people knowing God's truth important to you?

| Never | Seldom | On occasion | Often | Regularly |
|---|---|---|---|---|
|  |  |  |  |  |

8. Do you engage in apologetics (defense of the faith) in conversation?

| Never | Seldom | On occasion | Often | Regularly |
|---|---|---|---|---|
|  |  |  |  |  |

9. Does sin make you mad?

| Never | Seldom | On occasion | Often | Regularly |
|---|---|---|---|---|
|  |  |  |  |  |

10. Do you like theology?

| Never | Seldom | On occasion | Often | Regularly |
|---|---|---|---|---|
|  |  |  |  |  |

11. Are you a "Romans 12:2" person more often than a "Romans 12:15" one?

| Never | Seldom | On occasion | Often | Regularly |
|---|---|---|---|---|
|  |  |  |  |  |

12. Do you evangelize? Do you tell others about God's grace?

| Never | Seldom | On occasion | Often | Regularly |
|---|---|---|---|---|
|  |  |  |  |  |

## The PPK Model for Local Church Ministry

13. Do you seek out or maintain unbelieving friendships?

| Never | Seldom | On occasion | Often | Regularly |
|---|---|---|---|---|
|  |  |  |  |  |

14. Do you bring unbelieving friends to worship services?

| Never | Seldom | On occasion | Often | Regularly |
|---|---|---|---|---|
|  |  |  |  |  |

15. Think about going / been to the mission field?

| Never | Seldom | On occasion | Often | Regularly |
|---|---|---|---|---|
|  |  |  |  |  |

16. Do you write or read theological blog posts? Listen to podcasts of the same?

| Never | Seldom | On occasion | Often | Regularly |
|---|---|---|---|---|
|  |  |  |  |  |

17. Do you find yourself analyzing / correcting the preacher / teacher's view?

| Never | Seldom | On occasion | Often | Regularly |
|---|---|---|---|---|
|  |  |  |  |  |

18. Are you a "truth-hurts-so-be-in-pain" person?

| Never | Seldom | On occasion | Often | Regularly |
|---|---|---|---|---|
|  |  |  |  |  |

19. Does the slowness of people's change bother (or even anger) you?

| Never | Seldom | On occasion | Often | Regularly |
|---|---|---|---|---|
|  |  |  |  |  |

20. Do people's criticisms bother you?

| Never | Seldom | On occasion | Often | Regularly |
|---|---|---|---|---|
|  |  |  |  |  |

KEY: Never = 1, Seldom = 2, On Occasion = 3, Often = 4, Regularly = 5

Score: _____ /100

## PRIEST.

1. Do you weep or grieve over the suffering of your close people?

| Never (1) | Seldom (2) | On occasion (3) | Often (4) | Regularly (5) |
|---|---|---|---|---|
|  |  |  |  |  |

2. Read 1 Thessalonians 5:14. Do you find yourself more interested in "encouraging the fainthearted" than "admonishing the idle"?

| Never | Seldom | On occasion | Often | Regularly |
|---|---|---|---|---|
|  |  |  |  |  |

3. Do people tell you that you listen well?

| Never | Seldom | On occasion | Often | Regularly |
|---|---|---|---|---|
|  |  |  |  |  |

4. Do people seek you out for advice and counsel?

| Never | Seldom | On occasion | Often | Regularly |
|---|---|---|---|---|
|  |  |  |  |  |

5. Do times together with others sometimes turn into intimate conversations about life?

| Never | Seldom | On occasion | Often | Regularly |
|---|---|---|---|---|
|  |  |  |  |  |

6. Does sin make you sad?

| Never | Seldom | On occasion | Often | Regularly |
|---|---|---|---|---|
|  |  |  |  |  |

7. Have people told you that you are more people-oriented than task-oriented?

| Never | Seldom | On occasion | Often | Regularly |
|---|---|---|---|---|
|  |  |  |  |  |

8. Are you generally more patient and kind with people even in the face of their sins or sins against you?

| Never | Seldom | On occasion | Often | Regularly |
|---|---|---|---|---|
|  |  |  |  |  |

9. Are you a "Romans 12:15" person more often than a "Romans 12:2" one?

| Never | Seldom | On occasion | Often | Regularly |
|---|---|---|---|---|
|  |  |  |  |  |

10. Are you slow to confront but quick to encourage?

| Never | Seldom | On occasion | Often | Regularly |
|---|---|---|---|---|
|  |  |  |  |  |

## Part Three | The Paradigm in Action

11. Do you typically have a "longer view" of people and change? Are you more patient with others?

| Never | Seldom | On occasion | Often | Regularly |
|---|---|---|---|---|
|  |  |  |  |  |

12. Do you value finding creative ways to illustrate and apply biblical truths?

| Never | Seldom | On occasion | Often | Regularly |
|---|---|---|---|---|
|  |  |  |  |  |

13. Do you regularly seek time with believers?

| Never | Seldom | On occasion | Often | Regularly |
|---|---|---|---|---|
|  |  |  |  |  |

14. Are you eager to be hospitable?

| Never | Seldom | On occasion | Often | Regularly |
|---|---|---|---|---|
|  |  |  |  |  |

15. Do you counsel Scripture with others one-on-one or in small groups?

| Never | Seldom | On occasion | Often | Regularly |
|---|---|---|---|---|
|  |  |  |  |  |

16. Do believers' sins bother you enough to say something?

| Never | Seldom | On occasion | Often | Regularly |
|---|---|---|---|---|
|  |  |  |  |  |

## The PPK Model for Local Church Ministry

17. Are you engaged in "silent" ministries? "Behind the scenes" and like it that way?

| Never | Seldom | On occasion | Often | Regularly |
|---|---|---|---|---|
|  |  |  |  |  |

18. Are you fervent in prayer for the needs of the body of Christ?

| Never | Seldom | On occasion | Often | Regularly |
|---|---|---|---|---|
|  |  |  |  |  |

19. Are you in the church choir / band? Do you highly value music in worship?

| Never | Seldom | On occasion | Often | Regularly |
|---|---|---|---|---|
|  |  |  |  |  |

20. Do you use your money to support ministries a lot? Are you generous?

| Never | Seldom | On occasion | Often | Regularly |
|---|---|---|---|---|
|  |  |  |  |  |

KEY: Never = 1, Seldom = 2, On Occasion = 3, Often = 4, Regularly = 5

Score: _____ /100

## KING.

1. Do you excel (and enjoy) administrative tasks?

| Never (1) | Seldom (2) | On occasion (3) | Often (4) | Regularly (5) |
|---|---|---|---|---|
|  |  |  |  |  |

## Part Three | The Paradigm in Action

2. Are you burdened to find ways to facilitate ministry?

| Never | Seldom | On occasion | Often | Regularly |
|---|---|---|---|---|
|  |  |  |  |  |

3. Do you see the value in policies and procedures?

| Never | Seldom | On occasion | Often | Regularly |
|---|---|---|---|---|
|  |  |  |  |  |

4. Are you organized?

| Never | Seldom | On occasion | Often | Regularly |
|---|---|---|---|---|
|  |  |  |  |  |

5. Do you think and act according to organized systems?

| Never | Seldom | On occasion | Often | Regularly |
|---|---|---|---|---|
|  |  |  |  |  |

6. Does disorganization at church bother you?

| Never | Seldom | On occasion | Often | Regularly |
|---|---|---|---|---|
|  |  |  |  |  |

7. Do you get asked to be on church committees for business?

| Never | Seldom | On occasion | Often | Regularly |
|---|---|---|---|---|
|  |  |  |  |  |

8. Are you sensitive to the environment on Sunday mornings? Room setup, temperature, volume, etc.?

| Never | Seldom | On occasion | Often | Regularly |
|---|---|---|---|---|
|  |  |  |  |  |

## The PPK Model for Local Church Ministry

9. Do people say you are a "task person" more than a "people person"?

| Never | Seldom | On occasion | Often | Regularly |
|---|---|---|---|---|
| | | | | |

10. Do you want to make it easy for people to hear the Word of God?

| Never | Seldom | On occasion | Often | Regularly |
|---|---|---|---|---|
| | | | | |

11. Do you more often look for ways people can *do* things differently?

| Never | Seldom | On occasion | Often | Regularly |
|---|---|---|---|---|
| | | | | |

12. Can you manage money efficiently?

| Never | Seldom | On occasion | Often | Regularly |
|---|---|---|---|---|
| | | | | |

13. Are you organized with your time and ministry schedule?

| Never | Seldom | On occasion | Often | Regularly |
|---|---|---|---|---|
| | | | | |

14. Do you prefer studying Paul's epistles than the Psalms?

| Never | Seldom | On occasion | Often | Regularly |
|---|---|---|---|---|
| | | | | |

## Part Three | The Paradigm in Action

15. Are you often looking for teams (i.e., others who would supplement your ministry) to do ministry?

| Never | Seldom | On occasion | Often | Regularly |
|---|---|---|---|---|
|  |  |  |  |  |

16. Did you start a ministry or do you run its operations?

| Never | Seldom | On occasion | Often | Regularly |
|---|---|---|---|---|
|  |  |  |  |  |

17. Do you get frustrated when people don't "follow the plan"?

| Never | Seldom | On occasion | Often | Regularly |
|---|---|---|---|---|
|  |  |  |  |  |

18. Do you sometimes NOT know what to say or how to empathize?

| Never | Seldom | On occasion | Often | Regularly |
|---|---|---|---|---|
|  |  |  |  |  |

19. Are your mentoring relationships normally short (few weeks)?

| Never | Seldom | On occasion | Often | Regularly |
|---|---|---|---|---|
|  |  |  |  |  |

20. Would you rather follow the steps of church discipline (Matthew 18:15–17; cf. Titus 3:10–11) than Romans 12:2 or Galatians 6:2?

| Never | Seldom | On occasion | Often | Regularly |
|---|---|---|---|---|
|  |  |  |  |  |

KEY: Never = 1, Seldom = 2, On Occasion = 3, Often = 4, Regularly = 5

Score: _____ /100

## The PPK Model for Local Church Ministry

### EXPLAINING PPKa SCORES

Now that you've taken the questionnaire and have seen your scores, let's walk through the application of them.

**Prophet total:** _____

**Priest total:** _____

**King total:** _____

First, you probably noticed your scores were a range from the highest category (e.g., priest) to the lowest (e.g., king). This is normal and expected.[12] Jesus is the perfect balance of prophet, priest, and king. In other words, His scores would all be equal. That means He was a perfect, balanced mediator! We, however, are not perfect!

So, secondly, in the church, we believe God gives this balanced spread across the whole congregation. In other words, there are enough prophets, priests, and kings in any faithful congregation to build the kingdom of God as Jesus intends. In any given congregation, you will have to people who "live and die" to preach or teach the Word; you will have others who fervently pray for needs and encourage others in their faith; and you will have some who love to build, streamline, and maintain ministries.

This is freeing and encouraging because we can be confident that *our* job is to excel in the specific role or ministry God has given to us while He ensures others are doing their parts! Paul makes this point using the imagery of the body endowed by the Spirit with differing gifts (1 Cor 12):

> [4] Now there are varieties of gifts, but the same Spirit; [5] and there are varieties of service, but the same Lord; [6] and there are varieties of activities, but it is the same God who

---

12. It is sometimes true that a person's scores are close and no real "winner" is evident. This is where a trusted spiritual mentor or friend can help. Such a person should be consulted in order to clarify in what area a person with close scores can best serve.

empowers them all in everyone. [7] To each is given the manifestation of the Spirit for the common good. . . . [14] For the body does not consist of one member but of many. [15] If the foot should say, "Because I am not a hand, I do not belong to the body," that would not make it any less a part of the body. . . . [18] But as it is, God arranged the members in the body, each one of them, as he chose.

Each gift, like each individual body part, is essential to the functioning of the whole (just as Christ had to be a perfect balance of prophet, priest, and king to build His kingdom). God would not fail to give an adequate mixture of gifts in a local church for then it would not able to fulfill the commissions He has given.

Therefore, if your top score was "prophet" then you are more inclined to participate in ministries where you get to teach God's word. If it was "priest" then you are likely to be someone who "comes alongside" in prayer and service to others. If your top score was "king" then you are the kind of person who is concerned about ordering church so the prophets and priests can minister effectively.

## QUESTIONS FOR "TESTING" THE SCORES

A critical part of certifying the scores of the PPKa is accountability. Therefore, the test-taker should choose someone (an "evaluator") to evaluate scores who is in a position to be objective and knowledgeable about the person's record of ministry at the local church. These questions include:

1. Have you (the evaluator) read the definitions / expanded definitions used in the PPKa?
2. Does the ordered ranking of "prophet," "priest," and "king" according to the scores of the person accurately describe the ministry involvement of the test-taker?
3. Can you give examples to the test-taker of his ministry track record that confirms his scores?

4. If the scores do not match your experience of the test-taker's ministry, what corrective advice or guidance would you give? That is, can you provide examples that seem to contradict the test-taker's results or make him rethink how he has assessed himself?

Finding the "correct" score for some is easier than others. The PPKa is a self-directed tool that includes a trusted check by someone familiar with the test-taker and his ministry history. In the case of close scores, it may be true that exploring different ministry options is necessary to lead to the most fruitful ministry.

This should not be a high pressure scenario! The Lord is building His church with His people—gifting them as He needs. He will not hide His gifting of His saints though it might take some work to discern that area of ministry in some cases. Do not give up!

## SUGGESTED AREAS FOR MINISTRY

In this section, by example, the ministry of our local church is broken down by PPKa score so that a church member can immediately see where he or she might serve.[13]

## Welcome Ministry Volunteer

Priest—King
APPLICATION + ORGANIZATION
    Greeting team
    Hospitality team
    Refreshments team
    Bulletin distribution
    Sound team
    A/V team

---

13. Churches who use the PPKa would modify this list to suit their context.

Part Three | The Paradigm in Action

King—Priest
ORGANIZATION + APPLICATION
    Greeting team coordinator
    Hospitality area coordinator
    Refreshments coordinator
    Visitor care coordinator

## Children's Ministry Volunteer

Prophet—King
REVELATION + ORGANIZATION
    Elementary Sunday school class Teacher
    Parenting seminar teacher
    Curriculum advisor or reviewer

Prophet—Priest
REVELATION + APPLICATION
    Nursery worker
    Elementary small group leader
    Scripture memory teacher
    Special needs child class Teacher

Priest—Prophet
APPLICATION + REVELATION
    Children's church small group leader
    Class assistant
    Special needs child "buddy"

Priest—King
APPLICATION + ORGANIZATION
    Member of these teams:
        Elementary set-up team
        Nursery laundry team
        Refreshment team
        Greet team
        Craft preparation team

Toy distribution team
　　　Library maintenance team
　　　Shopping team
　　　Restocking team

King—Prophet
ORGANIZATION + REVELATION
　　　Department Team Leader

King—Priest
ORGANIZATION + APPLICATION
　　　Nursery Team leader
　　　Support team leader
　　　Volunteer coordinator

## Women's Ministry Volunteer

Prophet—King
REVELATION + ORGANIZATION
　　　Bible Teacher
　　　Event/Retreat Speaker
　　　Shepherdess (counseling / mentoring) Training Coordinator

Prophet—Priest
REVELATION + APPLICATION
　　　Small Group Leader
　　　Shepherdess
　　　Discussion Group Leader (Bible Studies)

Priest—Prophet
APPLICATION + REVELATION
　　　Small group leader
　　　Mentor of younger women
　　　Shepherdess
　　　Facilitator (Bible Studies)

Part Three | The Paradigm in Action

Priest—King
APPLICATION + ORGANIZATION
   Small group prayer coordinator
   Outing coordinator

King—Prophet
ORGANIZATION + REVELATION
   Director
   Curriculum evaluator

King—Priest
ORGANIZATION + APPLICATION
   Shepherdess Care Coordinator
   Bible Studies Coordinator
   Shepherdess Coordinator

## Men's Ministry Volunteer

Prophet—King
REVELATION + ORGANIZATION
   Bible Teacher
   Event/Retreat Speaker

Prophet—Priest
REVELATION + APPLICATION
   Small Group Leader
   Discussion Group Leader (Bible Studies)

Priest—Prophet
APPLICATION + REVELATION
   Mentor
   Facilitator (Bible Studies)

Priest—King
APPLICATION + ORGANIZATION
   Outing coordinator

## The PPK Model for Local Church Ministry

Prayer coordinator
Email coordinator

King—Prophet
ORGANIZATION + REVELATION
   Director
   Retreat Director

King—Priest
ORGANIZATION + APPLICATION
   Retreat coordinator
   Bible Studies Coordinator
   Small group co-leader

## Student Ministry Volunteer

Prophet—King
REVELATION + ORGANIZATION
   High School SBS teacher for large group ($9^{th}$-$12^{th}$ grades)
   Middle School SBS teacher for large group

Prophet—Priest
REVELATION + APPLICATION
   Senior High Small Group discipleship leader
   High School, middle school retreat small group leader
   Missions trip small group leader

Priest—Prophet
APPLICATION + REVELATION
   Encouragement partner
   Prayer Team member
   Youth Ministry Prayer Team member
   Senior High SBS leader/teacher (grade-specific)
   Middle School small group leader/teacher
   Media support
   VBS Worship leader

## Part Three | The Paradigm in Action

Priest—King
APPLICATION + ORGANIZATION
    Setup/clean-up crew member

King—Prophet
ORGANIZATION + REVELATION
    Sunday school teacher
    Mid-week ministry leaders
    Department Team Chair

King—Priest
ORGANIZATION + APPLICATION
    Chairman
    Hospitality leader
    High School, Middle School SBS Hospitality leader
    Refreshments Team leader
    Youth visitor assimilator

## Missions Ministry Volunteer

Prophet—King
REVELATION + ORGANIZATION
    Missions team curriculum writer
    Short term trip coordinator

Prophet—Priest
REVELATION + APPLICATION
    Missions team member (speaker)
    Partnership team member

Priest—Prophet
APPLICATION + REVELATION
    Artists for Missionary Care projects
    Missionary Care encouragers
    Prayer team

## The PPK Model for Local Church Ministry

Priest—King
APPLICATION + ORGANIZATION
    Missions Conference team member
    Missions team member
    Sewing team

King—Prophet
ORGANIZATION + REVELATION
    Department Chair
    Missions team leader

King—Priest
ORGANIZATION + APPLICATION
    Missions trip coordinator
    Writers to share our missionary stories

## Church Leadership

Prophet—King
REVELATION + ORGANIZATION
    Ruling elder
    Teaching elder

Prophet—Priest
REVELATION + APPLICATION
    Deacon

Priest—Prophet
APPLICATION + REVELATION
    Deacon

Priest—King
APPLICATION + ORGANIZATION
    Deacon
    Deacon assistant
    Session clerk
    Administrative staff

Part Three | The Paradigm in Action

<u>King—Prophet</u>
ORGANIZATION + REVELATION
    Ruling elder
    Teaching elder

<u>King—Priest</u>
ORGANIZATION + APPLICATION
    Ruling elder
    Diaconate chair

# CHAPTER SEVEN

## Conclusion

RICHARD BELCHER ASSERTS CHRISTIANS "tend to recognize the priestly role of believers but lack teaching on the significance of the prophet and king roles for the corporate church, her leaders, and individual believers."[1] His work on the "Prophet, Priest, and King" paradigm is significant for considering the church as ectypes, particularly in his discussion of the presence of the three offices in the Garden before the fall.[2]

The presence of the kingly role is found in the requirements inherent in Gen 1:26–28. With commands such as "subdue" and "have dominion," Gen 1:28 requires a royal, oversight role: "The function of human beings within God's creation is a royal one that is patterned after the God who created them."[3] Adam as priest in the Garden as nascent temple is grounded in his functions to

---

1. Belcher, *Prophet, Priest, and King*, 2016.
2. Others (e.g., à Brakel, *Reasonable Service*, 530) anchored the PPK roles of believers in the anointing of the Holy Spirit. Support for this can be found in the "knowledge," "righteousness," and "holiness" formulations of the *Westminster Confession* IV.2, the *Larger Catechism* question 17 and the *Shorter Catechism* question 10. In a complementary approach, Gladd unpacks the PPK in believers based on our union with Christ, *From Adam to Israel*, 116.
3. Belcher, *Prophet, Priest and King*, 6.

## Part Three | The Paradigm in Action

"guard" and "work."[4] And, Adam and Eve's response to and ministry of the Word as prophets can been seen in both the reception of God's command (Gen 2:16–17) as well as its incomplete repetition (Gen 3:3).[5]

In sum, as image-bearers, mankind had original responsibilities to manage and cultivate (king), to receive and pass along vibrant relationship with God (priest) and receive and give instruction according to God's initiative (prophet). Belcher points out the fall disrupted each of the functions of these roles. They were quickly proven to be incompetent with the word as prophets, both disobeying it and repeating it falsely. As priests, they no longer had direct access to God and now did their guarding and keeping work under judgment. And, as kings, their sin spoiled both their relationship to creation and oversight of it.[6]

Yet, as Dutch-American theologian R. B. Kuiper recognized in *The Glorious Body of Christ*, because of the individual anointing of the Holy Spirit of each person as "Christian," "Every single church member is at once a prophet, a priest and a king."[7]

The biblical data supporting these modern authors is in:

- The Lord established prophetic, priestly, and kingly types in Israel for the purpose of serving God and His people and giving glimpses of the one who was to come.

- Further, upon His coming, the Lord Jesus did His mediatorial ministry as the final prophet, the great high priest, and the

---

4. The same words are used to define the priests' work in the tabernacle: Numbers 3:7–8, 8:26 and 18:5–6; Belcher, *Prophet, Priest and King*, 9.

5. Belcher, *Prophet, Priest and King*, 9.

6. Belcher, *Prophet, Priest and King*, 11–12.

7. Kuiper, *Glorious Body*, 126. Edmund Clowney wrote, "All Christians, called to belong to Christ and equipped to serve him, hold office in his church. That office receives public recognition when a believer makes a public profession of faith and is welcomed by the church." Clowney, *The Church*, 207. Robert Peterson sees the continuation of the prophetic ministry of Christ, "A word should be said about the ministers through whom Christ performs His present prophetic ministry by the Spirit," Peterson, *Calvin and the Atonement*, 49.

## Conclusion

King of Kings—He holds these offices still and works in them in His exaltation.

- The Lord gave the church the tasks to continue His ministry and increase it in scope, reach and impact, making it "greater."

We have worked to understand the exegetical grounding of the church's pursuit of its mission in the offices of prophets, priests, and kings. Equipped with the PPKa, the church has the opportunity to identify, develop, and deploy gifted saints in these offices for the greater glory of Christ. May the Lord bless His people in our efforts to serve Him and glorify His name.

SDG.

# Bibliography

Allen, David L. *Hebrews*. Nashville: Broadman & Holman, 2010.
Arnold, Clinton. *Ephesians*. Grand Rapids: Zondervan, 2010.
Bauer, Walter, and F. Wilbur Gingrich. *A Greek-English Lexicon of the New Testament and Other Early Christian Literature*. Edited by William F. Arndt and Frederick W. Danker. 2nd edition. Chicago: University of Chicago Press, 1979.
Beale, G. K., and D. A. Carson. *The Temple and the Church's Mission: A Biblical Theology of the Dwelling Place of God*. Downers Grove, IL: IVP Academic, 2004.
Beale, Gregory K., and Donald A. Carson. *Commentary on the New Testament Use of the Old Testament*. Grand Rapids: Baker Academic, 2007.
Beasley-Murray, George R. *John*. Waco, TX: Word Books Publisher, 1987.
Beeke, Joel R., and Sinclair B. Ferguson, eds. *Reformed Confessions Harmonized*. Annotated edition. Grand Rapids: Baker Books, 1999.
Beeke, Joel, and Paul M. Smalley. *Reformed Systematic Theology, Volume 2: Man and Christ*. Wheaton, IL: Crossway Books, 2020.
Belcher, Richard. *Genesis: The Beginning of God's Plan of Salvation*. Fearn, Ross-shire, Scotland: Christian Focus, 2012.
———. *Prophet, Priest, and King: The Roles of Christ in the Bible and Our Roles Today*. Phillipsburg, NJ: P & R Publishing, 2016.
Bergen, Robert D. *1, 2 Samuel: An Exegetical and Theological Exposition of Holy Scripture*. Nashville: Broadman-Holman Publishers, 1996.
Berkhof, Louis. *Systematic Theology*. Grand Rapids: Eerdmans, 1996.
Bock, Darrell L. *Luke 1:1–9:50*. Grand Rapids: Baker Academic, 1996.
Borchert, Gerald. *John 12–21*. Nashville: Broadman & Holman, 2002.
Brakel, Wilhelmus A. *The Christian's Reasonable Service, Vol. 1*. Edited by Joel R. Beeke. Translated by Bartel Elshout. 5th Edition. Grand Rapids: Reformation Heritage Books, 1992.
Brannan, Rick. *Historic Creeds and Confessions*. Bellingham, WA: Lexham, 2001.
Breshears, Gerry. "The Body of Christ: Prophet, Priest or King?" *Journal of the Evangelical Theological Society* 37.1 (Mar 1994) 4–29.

# Bibliography

Bromiley, Geoffrey William. *Theological Dictionary of the New Testament Abridged in One Volume*. Edited by Gerhard Kittel, Geoffrey William Bromiley, and Gerhard Friedrich. Grand Rapids: Eerdmans, 1985.

Brown, Francis, S. R. Driver, Charles A. Briggs, and Wilhelm Gesenius. *The Brown-Driver-Briggs Hebrew and English Lexicon: Based on the Lexicon of William Gesenius*. Translated by Edward Robinson. Oxford: Clarendon, 1951.

Brown, Raymond. *The Message of Hebrews*. Downers Grove, IL: InterVarsity, 1982.

Bruce, F. F. *The Gospel and Epistles of John*. Grand Rapids: Eerdmans, 1983.

Calvin, John. *Commentaries on the Epistle of Paul the Apostle to the Hebrews*. Grand Rapids: Baker, 2009.

———. *Commentaries on the First Book of Moses Called Genesis*. Grand Rapids: Baker, 2009.

———. *Commentary on a Harmony of the Evangelists, Matthew, Mark and Luke*. Vol. 2. Grand Rapids: Baker, 2009.

———. *Commentary on the Book of Psalms*. Vol. 2. Grand Rapids: Baker, 2009.

———. *Commentary on the Epistle of Paul the Apostle to the Ephesians*. Grand Rapids: Baker, 2009.

———. *Institutes of the Christian Religion*. Edited by John T. McNeill. Translated by Ford Lewis Battles. Louisville: Westminster John Knox, 1960.

Calvin, John, and William Pringle. *Commentary on a Harmony of the Evangelists Matthew, Mark and Luke*. Vol. 2. Bellingham, WA: Logos Bible Software, 2010.

Carson, D. A. *The Gospel According to John*. Grand Rapids: Eerdmans Publishing, 1991.

Challies, Tim. "Spiritual Gift Assessments." Tim Challies (blog), Mar 25, 2004. https://www.challies.com/articles/spiritual-gift-assessments/.

———. "Spiritual Gift Assessment and the Bible." Tim Challies (blog), Jan 5, 2005. https://www.challies.com/articles/spiritual-gift-assessments-the-bible/.

Ciampa, Roy E., and Brian S. Rosner. *The First Letter to the Corinthians*. Grand Rapids: Eerdmans, 2010.

Currid, John D. *Deuteronomy*. First Edition. Evangelical Press Study Commentary. Darlington, UK; Webster, NY: Evangelical, 2006.

Edwards, Jonathan. *The Works of Jonathan Edwards*. Vol. 1. Peabody, MA: Hendrickson Publishers, Inc., 1998.

Elbert, Paul. "Calvin and the Spiritual Gifts." *Journal of the Evangelical Theological Society* 22.3 (1979): 235–56.

Ellingworth, Paul. *The Epistle to the Hebrews*. New International Greek Testament Commentary. Grand Rapids: Eerdmans, 1993.

Elwell, Walter A., ed. *Evangelical Dictionary of Biblical Theology*. Grand Rapids: Baker, 1996.

Elwell, Walter A., and Barry J. Beitzel, eds. *Baker Encyclopedia of the Bible*. 1st Edition. Grand Rapids: Baker, 1988.

Erickson, Millard J. *Christian Theology*. Grand Rapids: Baker, 1986.

# Bibliography

Fee, Gordon D. *God's Empowering Presence: The Holy Spirit in the Letters of Paul.* Grand Rapids: Baker Academic, 2009.

Ferguson, Sinclair B. *Let's Study Ephesians.* Carlisle, PA: Banner of Truth Trust, 2005.

Fowl, Stephen E. *Ephesians: A Commentary.* Edited by C. Clifton Black, M. Eugene Boring, and John T. Carroll. Louisville: Westminster John Knox, 2012.

France, R. T. *Jesus and the Old Testament.* Vancouver: Regent College Publishing, 1998.

Futato, Mark D. *Beginning Biblical Hebrew.* Winona Lake, IN: Eisenbrauns, 2003.

Gaebelein, Frank E., Dick Polcyn, Willem VanGemeren, Allen P. Ross, J. Stafford Wright, and Dennis F. Kinlaw. *The Expositor's Bible Commentary with the New International Version of the Holy Bible.* Vol. 5. Grand Rapids: Zondervan, 1991.

Garland, David E. *1 Corinthians.* Grand Rapids: Baker, 2003.

Geldenhuys, Norval. *The Gospel of Luke.* The New International Commentary on the New Testament. Grand Rapids: Eerdmans, 1977.

"Gifted2Serve—Online Spiritual Gifts Inventory—Welcome." http://buildingchurch.net/g2s.htm.

Gladd, Benjamin L. *From Adam and Israel to the Church.* Downers Grove, IL: InterVarsity; IVP Academic, 2019.

Gordon, T. David. "'Equipping' Ministry in Ephesians 4?" *Journal of the Evangelical Theological Society* 37.1 (March 1994) 70–78.

Green, Joel. *The Gospel of Luke.* Grand Rapids: Eerdmans, 1997.

Grudem, Wayne. *Systematic Theology: An Introduction to Biblical Doctrine.* Grand Rapids: Zondervan, 1994.

Guthrie, Donald. *Hebrews.* Grand Rapids: Eerdmans, 1983.

Hendriksen, William. *Galatians, Ephesians, Philippians, Colossians and Philemon.* Grand Rapids: Baker, 1962.

———. *The Gospel According to John: Two Volumes Complete in One.* Grand Rapids: Baker, 2002.

Hocking, David. *Spiritual Gifts: A Study Guide.* Orange, CA: Promise, 1992.

Hodge, Charles. *Commentary on Ephesians.* Electronic. Simpsonville, SC: Christian Classics Foundation, 1996.

———. *First and Second Corinthians.* Carlisle, PA: The Banner of Truth Trust, 1983.

———. *Systematic Theology.* Oak Harbor, WA: Logos Research Systems, Inc., 1997.

Houghton Mifflin Company. *The American Heritage Dictionary.* Boston: Houghton Mifflin Harcourt, 2012.

Jones, Timothy Paul. "Prophets, Priests and Kings Today? Theological and Practical Problems with the Use of the Munus Triplex as a Leadership Typology." *Perichoresis* 16.3 (2018): 63–86.

## Bibliography

Kidner, Derek. *Psalms 73–150*. Tyndale Old Testament Commentaries. Downers Grove, IL: InterVarsity, 1973.

Köstenberger, Andreas. *Signs of the Messiah: An Introduction to John's Gospel*. Bellingham, WA: Lexham, 2021.

———. "The Greater Works of the Believer According to John 14:1–12." *Didaskalia* 6.2 (Spring 1995) 36–45.

Kuiper, R. B. *The Glorious Body of Christ*. Edinburgh: Banner of Truth, 1967.

Kuyper, Abraham. *The Work of the Holy Spirit*. Chattanooga, TN: AMG, 2001.

Letham, Robert. *The Holy Trinity: In Scripture, History, Theology, and Worship, Revised and Expanded*. Phillipsburg, NJ: P & R, 2019.

Liddell, H.G. *A Lexicon: Abridged from Liddell and Scott's Greek-English Lexicon*. Oak Harbor, WA: Logos Research Systems, Inc., 1996.

Louw, Johannes P., and Eugene Albert Nida. *Greek-English Lexicon of the New Testament Based on Semantic Domains*. New York: United Bible Societies, 1996.

Mack, Wayne A, and David Swavely. *Life in the Father's House: A Member's Guide to the Local Church*. Phillipsburg, NJ: P & R, 2006.

Mackay, John L. *A Study Commentary on Isaiah Vol. 2, Vol. 2*. Darlington, UK: Evangelical, 2009.

Marshall, I. Howard. *The Gospel of Luke*. Grand Rapids: Eerdmans, 1978.

Marshall, Peyton, R. *The Measurement of Spiritual Gifts Using the Modified Houts Questionnaire*. Ann Arbor: University Microfilms, 1987.

McGraw, Ryan. "A Theology of Corporate Prayer: Preaching, Prayer Meetings and You." *Puritan Reformed Journal* 4.2 (Jul 2012) 170–80.

Milne, Bruce. *The Message of John*. Downers Grove, IL: InterVarsity, 1993.

Motyer, J. A. *Isaiah: An Introduction and Commentary*. Nottingham, UK; Downers Grove, IL: InterVarsity; IVP Academic, 2009.

O'Brien, Peter. *The Letter to the Ephesians*. Grand Rapids: Eerdmans, 1999.

Osborne, Grant. *Ephesians: Verse by Verse*. Bellingham, WA: Lexham, 2017.

———. *Luke: Verse by Verse*. Edited by Jeffrey Reimer, Elliot Ritzema, Danielle Thevenaz, and Awa Sarah. Bellingham, WA: Lexham, 2018.

Owen, John. *Epistle to the Hebrews*. Grand Rapids: Kregel, 1968.

———. *The Holy Spirit*. Edited by R. J. K. Law. Carlisle, PA: The Banner of Truth Trust, 1998.

Packer, J. I. *Concise Theology: A Guide to Historic Christian Beliefs*. Wheaton, IL: Tyndale House, 1993.

———. *Keep in Step with the Spirit: Finding Fullness in Our Walk with God*. Grand Rapids: Baker, 2005.

Paul, M.J. "The Order of Melchizedek (Ps 110:4 and Heb 7:3)." *Westminster Theological Journal* 49.1 (1987): 195–213.

Phillips, Richard. *Hebrews*. Phillipsburg, NJ: P & R, 2006.

Pink, Arthur W. *Gleanings in Genesis*. Chicago: Moody, 1981.

———. *The Holy Spirit*. Blacksburg, VA: Wilder, 2008.

Poythress, Vern S. *What Are Spiritual Gifts?* Phillipsburg, NJ: P & R, 2010.

# Bibliography

Presbyterian Church in America. *The Westminster Confession of Faith and Catechisms As Adopted By the Presbyterian Church in America with Proofs Texts.* Lawrenceville, GA: PCA Christian Education and Publications, 2007.

Ramsey, J. Michael. *The Gospel of John.* Grand Rapids: Eerdmans, 2010.

Riddlebarger, Kim. *First Corinthians.* Powder Springs, GA: Tolle Lege, 2013.

Sherman, Robert J. *King, Priest, and Prophet.* New York: T & T Clark, 2004.

"SPIRITUAL GIFTS ASSESSMENT." Aug 26, 2020. https://spiritualgiftsassessment.org.

"Spiritual Gifts Discovery Download." https://www.group.com/product/spiritual-gifts-discovery-download/1210000323712.

"Spiritual Gifts Test." https://giftstest.com.

Sproul, R. C. *The Purpose of God: Ephesians.* Fearn, Ross-shire, Scotland: Christian Focus, 1994.

Stein, Robert H. *Luke.* Nashville: Broadman, 2003.

Stott, John. *The Message of Ephesians.* Downers Grove, IL: InterVarsity, 1979.

Tasker, R. V. G. *John.* Grand Rapids: Eerdmans Publishing, 1960.

Thomas, Robert L., and W. Don Wilkins. *New American Standard Exhaustive Concordance of the Bible: Hebrew-Aramaic and Greek Dictionaries.* Updated. Anaheim: Foundation Publications Inc., 1998.

Ursinus, Zacharias. *The Commentary of Zacharias Ursinus on the Heidelberg Catechism.* Cincinnati: Elm Street Printing Company, 1888.

Vaughan, C. R. *The Gifts of the Holy Spirit.* Edinburgh: The Banner of Truth Trust, 1975.

Vincent, Marvin Richardson. *Word Studies in the New Testament.* Vol. 3. New York: Charles Scribner's Sons, 1887.

Visser t' Hooft, W. A. *The Kingship of Christ.* New York: Harper and Brothers, 1948.

Vos, Geerhardus J. *Reformed Dogmatics: Christology.* Translated by Richard B. Gaffin, Jr. Bellingham, WA: Lexham, 2014.

"Wagner-Modified Houts Questionnaire." https://trinityemc.com/spiritual-gifts.

Wagner, C. Peter. *Your Spiritual Gifts Can Help Your Church Grow.* Minneapolis: Chosen, 2017.

Wallace, Daniel B. *The Basics of New Testament Syntax.* Grand Rapids: Zondervan, 2000.

Warfield, Benjamin Breckinridge. *The Person and Work of the Holy Spirit.* Birmingham, AL: Solid Ground Christian Books, 2010.

Webb, Barry G. *Bible Speaks Today: Isaiah.* Downers Grove, IL: InterVarsity, 1997.

"Welcome to SHAPE." http://www.sbpcshape.org/.

Wilson, Geoffrey B. *Hebrews.* Carlisle, PA: Banner of Truth Trust, 1979.

Winslow, Octavius. *The Work of the Holy Spirit.* Carlisle, PA: Banner of Truth Trust, 1961.

Wood, D.R.W et al. *New Bible Dictionary.* Downers Grove, IL: InterVarsity, 1996.

www.ingramcontent.com/pod-product-compliance
Lightning Source LLC
Chambersburg PA
CBHW050809160426
43192CB00010B/1692